Dedication

To the leaders who choose accountability over convenience and governance over unchecked innovation.

MAXMETRICS® PROJECT LEADERSHIP SERIES

Moral Artificial Intelligence Projects

A Practical Guide to Building AI Systems That Deserve Trust

GLORIA J. MILLER

ATLANTA | HEIDELBERG

Moral Artificial Intelligence Projects

Published by Maxmetrics LLC, Atlanta, Georgia.

Library of Congress Control Number: 2026908031

International Standard Book Number:

979-8-9952095-6-0 Paperback United States

979-8-9952095-9-1 Paperback EU

979-8-9952095-7-7 ePub

979-8-9952095-8-4 Kindle

Preface

Artificial intelligence is no longer experimental. It is embedded in the systems that approve loans, detect fraud, recommend medical treatments, monitor security, and influence hiring decisions.

Yet most AI systems are not built in laboratories.

They are built in projects.

Over the past several years, I have studied and worked on issues of accountability in artificial intelligence projects. My research and professional experience have repeatedly pointed to the same conclusion: when AI systems cause harm, the failure is rarely just technical. It is usually a failure of governance, oversight, and responsibility.

Organizations often publish ethical principles. They adopt high-level guidelines. They speak about fairness and transparency. But when projects move from planning to deployment, those principles are rarely translated into operational controls.

Project teams are left managing complex systems with limited ethical structure.

This book was written to close that gap.

This is not a technical manual on algorithms or an abstract theoretical framework. It is a practical guide for leaders, project managers, sponsors, and governance professionals responsible for deploying AI systems in real-world organizations.

The book draws on scholarship across ethics, governance, and AI research, alongside my peer-reviewed work, including open-access publications (Miller, 2022a, 2022b, 2022c, 2025a, 2025b), and many years of professional practice in the field.

The central argument is simple: **AI projects are moral acts.**

When teams design, configure, deploy, and monitor AI systems, they make decisions that affect real people. Those decisions can produce benefit or harm. That makes project teams moral agents, whether they recognize it or not.

The goal of this book is to provide clarity.

You will find:

- A clear explanation of why ethics matters more in AI projects than in traditional IT.

- A structured framework for managing moral risk.

- Real-world examples of failure.

- Practical tools and checklists for implementation.

AI will continue to expand into critical areas of society. The question is not whether organizations will use AI.

The question is whether they will govern it responsibly.

This book is an invitation to lead that responsibility deliberately, rather than react once harm has already occurred.

Gloria J. Miller, DBA

Contents

I The Moral Foundation of AI Projects

II The Moral AI Project Framework

III   When AI Goes Wrong

IV   Implementation and Leadership

V   Closing and References

List of Figures

List of Tables

How to Use This Book

This book is written for practitioners responsible for designing, approving, managing, or overseeing artificial intelligence systems. It focuses on the governance and leadership structures required to ensure that AI systems are deployed responsibly. The guidance presented here combines research insights, regulatory expectations, and practical project management experience.

Who This Book Is For

Typical readers include:

Project and Program Managers

- Deliver AI-enabled systems

- Integrate governance checkpoints into project plans

- Balance technical progress with ethical accountability

Executives and Project Sponsors

- Approve funding and deployment decisions

- Carry ultimate accountability for system outcomes

- Require insight into governance risks

Data Scientists and AI Engineers

- Design and implement AI models

- Must understand how governance, data practices, and transparency requirements influence system design

Risk, Compliance, and Legal Professionals

- Interpret regulatory frameworks related to data governance or AI

- Assess readiness for responsible AI deployment

Policy and Governance Leaders

- Design internal AI governance frameworks

- Align innovation with regulatory and societal expectations

How the Book Is Organized

The chapters move from understanding the challenge to implementing practical governance solutions.

Part I: The Moral Foundation of AI Projects

Chapters 1–3: These chapters explain what artificial intelligence is, why AI systems create ethical and governance risks, and how traditional project success measures can fail to capture those risks.

Part II: The Moral AI Project Framework

Chapters 4–9: These chapters introduce the Five Pillars of Moral AI Projects and explain how each pillar addresses a specific governance risk. Practical guidance is provided for embedding these pillars into AI project decision-making. Each pillar chapter closes with a structured readiness checklist, organized by governance category, that teams can use during governance reviews and project gates.

Part III: When AI Goes Wrong

Chapters 10–15: These chapters examine real-world cases in which AI systems caused harm or sparked controversy. The cases illustrate how failures often originate in governance, data preparation, testing, or oversight rather than in the technology itself. Each case is connected to the pillar chapters to show which governance controls were absent or ineffective.

Part IV: Implementation and Leadership

Chapters 16–17: These chapters translate the framework into practical governance processes. They describe how organizations can integrate the Five Pillars into project lifecycles, governance checkpoints, and leadership structures. Leadership behavior, incentives, and organizational culture are examined as critical factors in sustaining responsible AI practices. Both chapters close with structured readiness checklists for implementation and leadership self-assessment.

Part V: Conclusion

The final chapter synthesizes the framework and emphasizes that responsible AI ultimately depends on leadership decisions.

Note for Technically Experienced Readers

Readers with a strong background in artificial intelligence, data science, or machine learning may wish to skim or skip portions of the early technical overview. Chapter 1 in particular provides a general introduction to artificial intelligence concepts and the evolution of AI systems, intended for readers less familiar with the technology. Those with prior experience may choose to move directly to the later chapters, which focus on governance, leadership, and project management practices for responsible AI deployment.

Tools in This Book

The book provides a set of practical tools that organizations can apply directly. They are designed to help translate abstract ethical principles into operational governance practices.

Readiness Checklists

Each of the five pillar chapters and both implementation chapters close with a structured readiness checklist organized by governance category. The checklists can be used during project reviews, governance gates, or leadership self-assessments and are the quickest entry point for practitioners who want an immediate diagnostic of their current governance position.

Appendix A: AI Governance Readiness Scoring Model

Provides a five-level maturity rubric covering two sections. Section 1 evaluates the strength of controls across the Five Pillars. Section 2 evaluates implementation and leadership maturity. Scores from both sections can be plotted on the governance matrix in the same appendix to identify the organization's current governance profile and priority areas for improvement.

Appendix B: AI Ethical Readiness Scorecard

Provides a structured worksheet for recording scores and evidence across the Five Pillars and the implementation and leadership dimensions assessed in Appendix A. Designed for use during formal governance reviews, project gates, and executive oversight discussions.

Appendix C: Stakeholder Identification and Inclusion Tool

Provides a structured register and representation-planning tool for identifying stakeholders across the AI lifecycle, assessing influence and potential harm, and defining representation mechanisms for underrepresented and low-voice groups.

Appendix D: Dataset Governance Assessment

Supports evaluation of whether data collection is responsible, proportionate, and justified. Covers representativeness, inclusion and exclusion risks, bias considerations, and the governance questions teams should ask before treating any dataset as fit for purpose. It is designed to be used alongside the Dataset Governance worksheet in Appendix E.

Appendix E: AI System Documentation Worksheets

Provides four one-page worksheets, supported by an ecosystem overview diagram, that together create a record of how an AI system is designed, built, deployed, and monitored. The Dataset Governance worksheet is designed to be used alongside the Dataset Governance Assessment in Appendix D.

Introduction

A customer walks into a retail store. A camera scans her face. An alert appears on a screen.

Within minutes, she is followed by staff, questioned, and asked to leave.

The system worked exactly as designed. The project that deployed it was delivered on time. The technology functioned. And yet, harm occurred.

This is the ethical gap in artificial intelligence projects.

This case is examined in Chapter 11.

The New Reality of AI Decisions

Artificial intelligence systems now influence decisions that affect people's access to:

- Financial services

- Employment opportunities

- Healthcare treatment

- Insurance coverage

- Public safety

Unlike traditional software, AI systems do more than store information or automate routine processes.

They evaluate, classify, predict, and recommend.

They shape outcomes.

In many cases, their outputs directly influence how people are treated.

When decisions carry consequences, they carry moral weight.

Why Traditional Project Success Is Not Enough

Most organizations measure project success using three criteria:

- Was it delivered on time?

- Was it delivered within budget?

- Did it meet functional requirements?

These measures are necessary.

But for AI systems, they are not sufficient.

An AI project can meet all traditional success metrics and still:

- Produce unfair outcomes

- Reinforce hidden bias

- Cause reputational damage

- Trigger regulatory enforcement

- Harm vulnerable individuals

Technical correctness does not guarantee ethical defensibility.

The Accountability Problem

AI systems operate at scale.

A small design decision can affect thousands of people.

A minor bias can multiply across millions of transactions.

When harm occurs, responsibility is often unclear.

Is it the developer? The vendor? The project manager? The sponsor? The executive who approved deployment?

Delegating decisions to a system does not eliminate accountability.

It redistributes it.

Without clear governance, responsibility becomes diluted.

And when responsibility is diluted, harm becomes easier to ignore.

Closing the Ethical Gap

The ethical gap emerges when:

- AI systems influence high-stakes outcomes

- Projects focus on delivery rather than impact

- Ethical principles exist but are not operationalized

- Accountability is not clearly assigned

Closing this gap requires more than good intentions.

It requires structure.

This book provides that structure.

The Framework for the Five Pillars of Moral AI Projects

Responsible AI does not emerge from technology alone.

It emerges from leadership, governance, and disciplined project execution.

Figure 1 illustrates the framework used throughout this book.

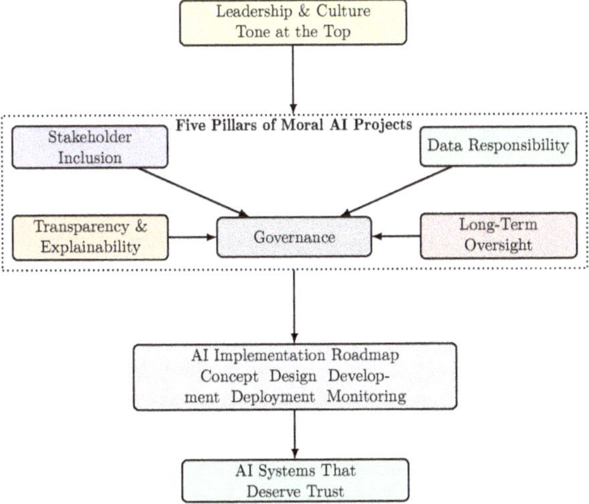

Figure 1: The Book's Orientation Overview. Framework for Moral AI Projects. Ethical leadership establishes governance structures that integrate the five pillars into the AI project lifecycle, producing systems that deserve trust.

At the top sits **ethical leadership**. Leadership establishes the tone that determines whether governance is taken seriously or treated as a formality.

Below leadership sits **governance**. Governance defines decision rights, assigns accountability, and establishes escalation routes when risks emerge.

Surrounding governance are four operational pillars:

- Stakeholder Inclusion

- Data Responsibility

- Transparency and Explainability

- Long-Term Oversight

These pillars embed ethical safeguards directly into the AI project lifecycle.

Projects move through phases of concept definition, design, development, deployment, and monitoring.

When leadership, governance, and these pillars are integrated into the lifecycle, the result is the outcome shown at the bottom of the framework:

AI systems that deserve trust.

Trustworthy systems are not the product of technical performance alone.

They are the result of responsible leadership, disciplined governance, and continuous oversight.

What This Book Provides

The chapters that follow translate these ideas into practical guidance.

You will find:

- Explanations of why AI projects create new governance risks

- A structured framework for responsible AI project delivery

- Analysis of real-world failures

- Tools and checklists to assess ethical readiness

AI innovation is accelerating.

The question is not whether organizations will deploy AI systems.

The question is whether those systems will be deployed responsibly.

Part I

The Moral Foundation of AI Projects

Chapter 1

Understanding Artificial Intelligence

Artificial intelligence is one of the most discussed technologies today. It is also one of the most misunderstood.

The term "artificial intelligence" does not describe a single technology. Instead, it refers to a broad group of computational methods that help machines perform tasks normally associated with human intelligence.

These tasks include recognizing patterns, understanding language, identifying images, making predictions, or assisting with decisions.

Because AI includes many different technologies and applications, it is best understood as an evolving umbrella term rather than a single defined system.

Understanding this complexity is important for leaders who must manage and govern AI projects responsibly.

Artificial Intelligence as an Umbrella Term

The meaning of artificial intelligence often depends on context.

In some situations, it refers to systems that perform specific intelligent tasks, such as speech recognition or fraud detection. In others, it refers to a broader field of research and engineering focused on building machines capable of performing complex cognitive tasks.

Public discussions sometimes frame AI as a technology that may replace human work or achieve human-like intelligence. However, many researchers describe it more simply as a collection of tools that support decision-making, automation, and information processing.

For the purposes of responsible project leadership, artificial intelligence can be understood as:

> Systems that use data, models, and algorithms to perform tasks associated with human intelligence, such as language processing, pattern recognition, or adaptive decision-making.

This definition highlights three key elements:

- The data used to train or guide the system

- The algorithms and models that process that data

- The ability to apply learned patterns to perform tasks

This definition encompasses many technologies commonly grouped under the AI label, such as machine learning, natural language processing, large language models, computer vision, and generative models.

Because these technologies continue to evolve, the meaning of AI also evolves with them.

The Evolution of AI Systems

Artificial intelligence has developed over many decades.

Early AI systems were often rule-based programs known as expert systems. These systems used predefined rules to solve narrow problems, such as diagnosing equipment failures or recommending financial actions.

Although these systems automated some tasks, they had clear limitations. They could not easily adapt to new situations. They also struggled to explain their reasoning in ways users could understand.

As computing power increased and large datasets became available, new types of AI systems emerged.

Machine learning systems use statistical methods to identify patterns in large datasets. These patterns are then used to make predictions or recommendations.

Machine learning is now widely used in areas such as fraud detection, credit scoring, and recommendation systems.

More recently, generative AI systems have gained prominence. These systems can produce new content—such as text, images, audio, or video—in response to user prompts.

Examples include language models such as ChatGPT and BERT, and image-generation systems such as DALL–E.

These models are trained on very large datasets. They learn patterns in language or images and generate outputs accordingly.

Because these systems can be applied across many industries, they are often described as general-purpose technologies.

However, wide applicability does not mean these systems act independently. Most current AI systems remain tools that support human work rather than systems that pursue goals of their own.

Emerging Forms of Agentic AI

A newer concept in AI research is *agentic AI.*

Agentic systems are designed to pursue goals by performing sequences of tasks. They may gather information, plan actions, and adjust their strategies based on new data.

Instead of responding only to direct instructions, these systems attempt to complete broader objectives.

In theory, this allows them to operate with less continuous human supervision.

While such capabilities are still developing, they raise important governance questions.

If a system can take actions on its own, determining who is accountable for outcomes becomes more complex. Developers design the system, organizations deploy it, and users interact with it. As systems gain greater autonomy, responsibility for outcomes remains with the people who build, deploy, and use the system. However, accountability may become harder to attribute across these roles.

Importantly, greater autonomy does not automatically produce stronger accountability. In practice, accountability depends less on how a system is labeled than on governance design, oversight mechanisms, and the specific capabilities and risks involved.

Responsible AI governance must therefore evaluate what a system actually does and what risks it poses, rather than relying on terms like "autonomous" or "agentic."

Automation and the AI Continuum

Another important feature of artificial intelligence is the level of automation.

AI systems can operate at many different levels.

Some systems simply provide information to support human decisions. Others perform tasks automatically that were once done by people.

Researchers often describe automation along a continuum.

At the lowest level, there is no automation. Humans perform all tasks.

At intermediate levels, systems provide decision support or partial automation. Humans still review results and make final decisions.

At the highest levels, systems may perform tasks without direct human involvement.

Table 1.1 summarizes a widely used framework that describes ten levels of automation. It was first developed for autonomous vehicles and systems used in hazardous environments.

The appropriate level of automation depends on the type of task being performed.

Table 1.1: Levels of Automation

Level	Role of the AI System
1	No automation. Humans make all decisions and take all actions.
2	The system lists many possible options. The human chooses what to do.
3	The system suggests a few options. The human chooses the final action.
4	The system recommends one option. The human decides whether to follow it.
5	The system prepares an action and carries it out only if the human approves.
6	The system prepares an action and will carry it out unless the human stops it within a short time.
7	The system makes and carries out the decision, then tells the human what it did.
8	The system makes and carries out the decision and reports it if the human asks.
9	The system makes and carries out the decision and informs the human only in selected situations.
10	Full autonomy. The system makes all decisions and acts without human involvement.

Source: (adapted from Sheridan & Verplank, 1978)

Stable, well-defined tasks may allow higher levels of automation. Tasks involving uncertainty, ethical judgment, or public risk generally require stronger human oversight.

Automation can improve efficiency and consistency. However, it can also introduce new risks.

Users may rely too heavily on automated results. Engineers may underestimate system limitations. Organizations may deploy systems before they are adequately tested.

Errors can arise from many sources, including system design, data quality, user behavior, or management decisions.

Responsible governance means recognizing these risks and building appropriate safeguards into AI projects from the outset.

Debates About Human-Level Intelligence

Public discussions about AI often focus on whether machines will one day achieve human-level intelligence.

Some researchers describe a progression from narrow AI systems, systems designed for specific tasks, to artificial general intelligence (AGI), which could perform a wide range of cognitive tasks.

At the far end of this spectrum lies artificial superintelligence, which would exceed human abilities across many domains.

These possibilities raise important questions about governance and control.

However, many scholars argue that current AI systems remain far from human-like intelligence.

Large language models, for example, generate text by predicting likely word sequences based on patterns in data.

They do not understand language in the way humans do.

These systems can produce convincing responses, but they can also generate incorrect or fabricated information.

For this reason, many experts view current AI systems as advanced tools rather than systems capable of independent thought.

Human Responsibility in AI Systems

Despite ongoing debates about the future of AI, one point remains clear.

Humans remain responsible for the design, development, and deployment of AI systems.

Engineers build models. Organizations decide how systems are used. Managers establish governance and oversight.

AI systems do not operate outside human decision-making.

This has important implications for accountability.

When an AI system produces harmful outcomes, responsibility does not disappear.

Instead, it must be traced across the network of actors involved.

Developers may be responsible for system design. Organizations may be responsible for deployment decisions. Operators may be responsible for monitoring system performance.

As AI systems become more complex and autonomous, defining responsibility becomes more challenging but also more important.

Autonomy does not dissolve accountability automatically. Strong accountability must be deliberately designed through governance structures, clear decision rights, and meaningful oversight.

Why Understanding AI Matters for Leadership

AI systems differ widely in their capabilities, risks, and levels of automation. Understanding those differences is essential for responsible leadership.

Some systems support decisions. Others automate tasks. Some may eventually operate with greater independence.

Because of this diversity, leaders must treat AI as a category of technologies rather than a single tool.

Responsible leadership begins with understanding what these systems are and what they are not.

They are powerful tools that can support innovation and decision-making.

But they remain part of human organizations.

Their outcomes ultimately reflect the choices of the people who design, deploy, and govern them.

AI systems combine automation, data-driven learning, and decision influence. These characteristics introduce new ethical questions about responsibility, fairness, and oversight.

The next chapter examines why these characteristics create an ethical gap in many AI projects and why conventional approaches to project governance are often insufficient.

Chapter 2

The Ethical Gap in AI Projects

AI systems are not neutral tools.

They make decisions. They influence outcomes. They create benefits for some and harm for others.

To understand the ethical gap in AI projects, we must first understand two foundational ideas: morality and ethics.

What Is a Moral Issue?

A moral issue exists when a decision or action has consequences for others.

If a choice can cause harm or produce benefit, it carries moral weight.

Every moral decision involves three elements:

- A choice

- An actor making that choice

- Consequences that affect others

Many decisions have a moral component, even when the decision-maker does not recognize it.

When a project team selects a dataset, sets a model parameter, or approves deployment, those actions can affect thousands or even millions of people.

That makes them moral decisions.

Morality and Ethics: Are They Different?

In everyday language, the two words are often used interchangeably.

For practical purposes in AI projects:

- **Morality** refers to judgments about right and wrong.

- **Ethics** refers to the standards, principles, and rules that guide moral behavior.

An ethical decision is one that aligns with accepted moral and legal standards.

An unethical decision violates those standards.

Some philosophers argue that instead of asking whether something is "right" or "wrong," we should ask:

- Is this action unjust in itself?

- Or is it unjust given the circumstances?

This shifts responsibility to the decision-maker. It requires reasonable judgment.

In AI projects, that judgment cannot be avoided simply because a system performs the action.

Delegating a decision to a machine does not remove moral responsibility from the humans involved.

Are Machines Moral Agents?

AI systems can act with autonomy. They can recommend, predict, approve, deny, classify, and prioritize.

However, machines do not possess moral awareness.

They do not understand justice or fairness.

They operate according to the parameters and data provided to them.

Some scholars argue that machines should demonstrate qualities such as:

- Robustness

- Consistency

- Universality

- Simplicity

But even where machines meet these standards, responsibility still traces back to humans.

AI systems are artificial agents.

They are not moral agents in the human sense.

Project Teams as Moral Agents

A moral agent is someone who makes decisions that affect others, even if they do not recognize the moral dimension at the time.

AI project teams meet this definition.

Consider the decisions made during an AI project:

- Choosing what data to include

- Selecting development methods

- Setting model thresholds

- Designing user interfaces

- Determining deployment timing

- Approving automation levels

Each of these choices can produce harm or benefit.

Therefore, AI project teams are moral agents.

They cannot claim neutrality.

Autonomy, Knowledge, and Responsibility

Moral responsibility increases when two conditions are present:

1. The actor understands the potential consequences.
2. The actor has the autonomy to influence outcomes.

AI professionals often possess specialized knowledge. They understand model limitations, bias risks, and technical trade-offs better than clients or users.

This knowledge increases their moral responsibility.

At the same time, full foresight is impossible.

No modeler can predict every future use or misuse of a system.

This creates ethical complexity.

But uncertainty does not eliminate responsibility.

It increases the need for caution.

Why Principles Alone Are Not Enough

Over the past decade, many AI ethics guidelines have been published.

Common principles include:

- Transparency

- Fairness

- Non-maleficence (do no harm)

- Privacy

- Responsibility

- Trust

These principles are important.

But principles alone do not change behavior.

The challenge is translation.

How do you turn "fairness" into a concrete design choice? How do you turn "transparency" into project documentation standards?

There is no automatic bridge between values and implementation.

Ethics must be embedded into governance structures, decision checkpoints, and accountability systems.

Why Morality and Ethics Matter More in AI Projects

All technology projects have consequences.

But AI projects amplify those consequences.

Traditional IT systems typically store information, automate workflows, or support human decisions. AI systems increasingly make or heavily influence decisions.

That difference changes the moral stakes.

1. AI Systems Influence Human Outcomes Directly

An accounting system records transactions. A document management system stores files.

An AI system can:

- Approve or deny a loan

- Flag a person as high risk

- Recommend medical treatment

- Filter job candidates

- Trigger law enforcement attention

These are not minor operational tasks.

They affect individuals' livelihoods, health, reputation, and freedom.

When systems influence life outcomes, moral responsibility increases.

2. AI Operates at Scale

Many traditional IT systems are limited to a department or organization.

AI systems can operate globally.

Once deployed:

- Decisions are repeated thousands or millions of times.

- Small biases are multiplied.

- Errors scale instantly.

A flawed human decision affects one person at a time.

A flawed AI decision can affect thousands within minutes.

Scale magnifies ethical risk.

3. AI Can Reduce Human Oversight

Some AI systems operate with minimal human intervention.

Automation can increase efficiency.

But it can also reduce reflection.

When humans are removed from real-time decision-making:

- Errors may go unnoticed.

- Harm may persist longer.

- Accountability may become unclear.

Delegating decisions to machines does not remove moral responsibility; it increases the need for governance and oversight.

Without deliberate governance mechanisms, higher automation can instead widen accountability gaps.

4. AI Depends on Data That Reflects Society

AI systems learn from historical data.

That data may contain:

- Past discrimination

- Incomplete representation

- Cultural bias

- Structural inequality

Unlike traditional rule-based systems, AI models can absorb and reproduce patterns embedded in that data.

Without ethical scrutiny, systems risk automating injustice.

5. AI Systems Can Become Black Boxes

Some AI models function as "black boxes."

Even developers may not fully understand how a complex model arrives at a specific prediction.

When decisions cannot be clearly explained:

- Trust declines

- Appeals become difficult

- Accountability becomes blurred

Black-box systems increase ethical pressure.

If a decision affects a person, that person deserves an explanation.

6. AI Can Cause Significant Harm

Most IT systems cause inconvenience when they fail.

AI systems can cause:

- Financial exclusion

- Medical misdiagnosis

- Unfair surveillance

- Reputational damage

- Social inequality

In extreme cases, harm can be severe or even life-threatening.

The severity of these potential outcomes raises the moral threshold for every project decision.

The Ethical Intensity of AI Projects

Moral intensity increases when:

- Consequences are significant

- Many people are affected

- Harm is difficult to reverse

- Responsibility is diffuse

AI projects often meet all four conditions.

That is why ethics cannot be treated as an optional layer added after development.

In AI projects, ethics is not a compliance exercise.

It is a core design requirement.

When systems make or influence decisions about people, project teams must operate with heightened moral awareness.

AI projects do not merely deploy software.

They shape social outcomes.

And that makes ethical leadership essential.

The Ethical Gap Defined

The ethical gap in AI projects appears when technical success is mistaken for moral success.

It occurs when:

- Responsibility is assumed to lie with the system.

- Ethical reflection is separated from project management.

- Governance focuses only on time, cost, and scope.

- Moral consequences are treated as secondary effects.

An AI model can be accurate and still be unjust.

A system can be efficient and still cause harm.

A project can meet every contractual goal and still fail ethically.

The gap exists because AI decisions are often delegated to systems, while accountability remains with humans.

But delegation does not remove responsibility.

It redistributes it.

Project Teams as Ethical Decision-Makers

AI project teams do not simply build technology.

They:

- Define system capabilities

- Select data boundaries

- Set thresholds for decisions

- Determine levels of automation

- Approve deployment timing

These are not neutral technical choices.

They are moral choices with real-world consequences.

Recognizing project teams as moral agents changes how AI projects must be managed.

It means ethics cannot be an afterthought.

It must be built into governance, decision checkpoints, and leadership accountability.

Closing the Ethical Gap

Closing the ethical gap requires three commitments:

1. Acknowledge that AI projects involve moral decisions.
2. Assign clear accountability for those decisions.
3. Embed ethical review into the project lifecycle.

Ethical AI is not achieved by publishing principles.

It is achieved by structuring responsibility.

When project teams accept their role as moral agents, AI projects move from technical execution to responsible leadership.

And that is the foundation for building systems that deserve trust.

If AI project success requires governance, accountability, stakeholder protection, and ongoing oversight, then leaders need a structured way to embed these safeguards into project practice.

The following chapters introduce the governance framework designed to operationalize these responsibilities.

Chapter 3

Redefining AI Project Success

Even when organizations recognize that humans remain responsible for AI systems, responsibility in practice is often fragmented or unclear.

Research into accountability patterns in AI projects confirms this: responsibility tends to be fragmented, overlapping, and selectively applied. Even when roles are formally assigned, operational accountability does not consistently align with documented structures (Miller, 2025c).

This structural reality has direct implications for how success should be defined.

Traditional project management defines success in terms of:

- Schedule performance

- Budget adherence

- Scope completion

These remain necessary conditions, but they are no longer sufficient.

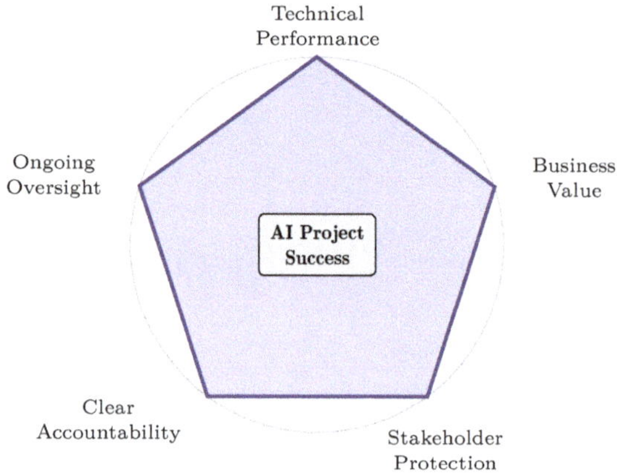

Figure 3.1: Five Dimensions of AI Project Success

3.1 Five Dimensions of AI Project Success

AI project success must be evaluated across five interdependent dimensions:

1. Technical performance
2. Business value
3. Stakeholder protection
4. Clear accountability
5. Ongoing oversight

These dimensions respond directly to observed governance weaknesses in AI project environments.

If any one dimension collapses, the success of the project as a whole is compromised.

Table 3.1: Five Dimensions of AI Project Success

Dimension	What It Requires
Technical Performance	Validated accuracy, robustness, monitoring
Business Value	Sustainable benefit, risk-controlled returns
Stakeholder Protection	Bias testing, privacy safeguards
Clear Accountability	Named decision rights and escalation routes
Ongoing Oversight	Continuous monitoring and retraining governance

3.2 Technical Performance

Technical performance extends beyond initial system functionality.

In many AI projects, responsibility for technical validation is spread across several roles; project owners, managers, and teams each assume partial responsibility.

However, no single role consistently maintains end-to-end performance accountability. When ownership is fragmented in this way, important risks can be overlooked.

This fragmentation increases risk.

Technical integrity therefore requires:

- Rigorous validation prior to deployment
- Testing under realistic operating conditions

- Clear ownership of accuracy metrics

- Ongoing monitoring of system behavior

Performance is not a milestone.

It is a maintained condition.

3.3   Business Value

AI initiatives are typically justified by efficiency gains, automation benefits, or financial returns.

Research indicates that accountability for financial gains tends to align with formal organizational roles. However, such alignment does not consistently translate into overall project success.

Classic project trade-offs remain:

- Faster delivery may weaken cost control.

- Short-term gains may increase long-term risk exposure.

Business value in AI projects must therefore be understood as sustainable value, not isolated financial metrics.

It includes:

- Durable strategic advantage

- Controlled risk exposure

- Long-term operational capability

- Balanced cost-benefit realization

A project that improves quarterly performance while increasing regulatory vulnerability cannot be considered fully successful.

3.4 Stakeholder Protection

Research shows that no single role consistently assumes responsibility for regulatory compliance, sustainability, or societal impact in AI projects.

Instead, these responsibilities are often distributed unevenly and sometimes neglected entirely.

This diffusion becomes particularly problematic when AI systems expand decision influence or operate with limited transparency.

Stakeholder protection therefore requires:

- Formal bias and fairness assessment

- Privacy and data governance safeguards

- Environmental and sustainability evaluation

- Explicit compliance accountability

Importantly, autonomy labels alone do not predict stronger accountability in these areas.

Governance demands increase when system capabilities expand decision reach, introduce hidden logic, or elevate operational risk.

Success must therefore be calibrated to actual system capability rather than autonomy classification.

These protections correspond directly to core elements of responsible AI governance, including stakeholder inclusion, data responsibility, and transparency.

3.5   Clear Accountability

Formal accountability assignments do not automatically produce operational accountability.

Research shows that project owners, managers, and teams each assume fewer than half of the responsibilities theoretically associated with their roles. The remainder is distributed without a consistent primary steward.

Under delivery pressure, accountability does not reallocate cleanly.

It erodes.

In particular:

- Accountability for ethical practices declines.

- Compliance oversight weakens.

- Transparency responsibilities diminish.

This erosion reflects a structural tension between speed and governance.

Clear accountability requires:

- Explicit authority to intervene

- Defined escalation pathways

- Cross-role coordination

- Protection of compliance and ethics from delivery trade-offs

Accountability must be actively maintained.

It does not sustain itself.

3.6 Ongoing Oversight

AI systems introduce dynamic governance demands.

Research shows that simple classifications—autonomous versus non-autonomous—do not reliably predict the strength of accountability.

Instead, accountability structures must evolve as system capabilities expand.

Projects incorporating generative or agentic features, which increase decision reach and introduce hidden reasoning processes, generate greater coordination and governance complexity.

Without sustained oversight:

- Monitoring weakens

- Performance deviations accumulate

- Governance misalignment increases

- Compliance risks grow

Delivery pressure further amplifies these risks by weakening oversight in areas not directly tied to short-term performance metrics.

Ongoing oversight therefore includes:

- Continuous performance auditing

- Periodic compliance review

- Sustainability monitoring

- Transparent reporting mechanisms

Deployment is not the end of responsibility.

It is the beginning of operational accountability.

3.7   A Refined Definition of AI Project Success

Drawing on both practical experience and empirical research, AI project success can be defined as:

> *The delivery of an AI system that achieves sustainable business value while maintaining technical reliability, protecting affected stakeholders, ensuring enforceable accountability structures, and sustaining governance oversight throughout its lifecycle.*

This definition reflects several important realities:

- Formal role alignment alone does not ensure accountability in practice.

- Increased system capability increases governance complexity.

- Delivery pressure selectively weakens oversight.

- Success is multidimensional and evolves over time.

AI project success is therefore not a binary outcome.

It is a balanced configuration across interdependent domains.

3.8 The Practical Implication

Organizations cannot rely solely on:

- Role charts

- Autonomy labels

- Ethical principle statements

- Delivery metrics

They must design governance structures that:

- Align accountability with actual system capabilities

- Protect oversight under delivery pressure

- Integrate compliance into project workflows

- Sustain monitoring beyond launch

Redefining success is not conceptual refinement.

It is operational necessity.

Without it, AI projects may meet contractual objectives while failing strategically, legally, or socially.

That is not success.

Part II

The Moral AI Project Framework

Chapter 4

The Five Pillars of Moral AI Projects

From Principles to Practice

Ethical AI does not emerge from intention alone.

It requires structure.

Earlier chapters examined why AI projects create moral risk and why traditional project success measures are insufficient. The question now becomes practical:

How should organizations structure AI projects to make ethics operational?

The answer is not a single policy, checklist, or technical safeguard.

It is a system of governance.

This system is built on five reinforcing pillars.

Overview of the Framework

Pillars

The framework introduced in this book rests on five pillars:

1. Governance
2. Stakeholder Inclusion
3. Data Responsibility
4. Transparency and Explainability
5. Long-Term Oversight

Each pillar addresses a distinct dimension of moral risk.

Together, they create ethical stability.

No single pillar is sufficient on its own.

Governance without transparency becomes control without clarity. Transparency without data responsibility becomes explanation without integrity. Data responsibility without inclusion becomes technical fairness without representation. Oversight without governance becomes monitoring without authority.

The pillars are interdependent.

Relationship to Existing AI Frameworks and Regulations

The Five Pillars framework does not exist in isolation.

Over the past several years, governments and standards organizations have developed important guidance for responsible AI.

Three influential examples are worth noting:

- **The NIST AI Risk Management Framework (AI RMF)** provides structured guidance for identifying, measuring, and managing AI risks across the system lifecycle, emphasizing trustworthiness characteristics such as safety, fairness, transparency, and accountability (Tabassi, 2023).

- **ISO/IEC 42001**, the international standard for AI Management Systems, defines governance structures, organizational roles, and lifecycle controls for responsible AI deployment and monitoring (International Standards Organization, 2023).

- **The European Union AI Act** establishes a legally binding risk-based regulatory regime that classifies AI systems by risk level and imposes obligations for high-risk applications (European Union, 2024).

These frameworks represent significant advances in AI governance.

Other jurisdictions are also developing their own approaches, including national AI strategies, sector-specific regulations, and regional governance frameworks.

While regulatory frameworks often classify systems by autonomy or risk characteristics, stronger accountability does not arise from classification alone. Effective accountability emerges only when regulatory expectations are translated into concrete governance controls tied to system capabilities, use context, and operational risk.

Standards, Regulation, and Project Governance

Most existing frameworks operate at the level of regulation, policy, and enterprise risk management.

However, AI systems are ultimately created within projects.

Project leadership must translate regulatory expectations, risk management guidance, and organizational policies into concrete design decisions, development practices, and oversight mechanisms.

The Five Pillars framework operates at this project governance layer, connecting regulatory and standards expectations to the practical realities of AI system development.

Figure 4.1 illustrates this relationship.

The Five Pillars serve as the operational bridge between high-level governance frameworks and the day-to-day decisions made within AI projects.

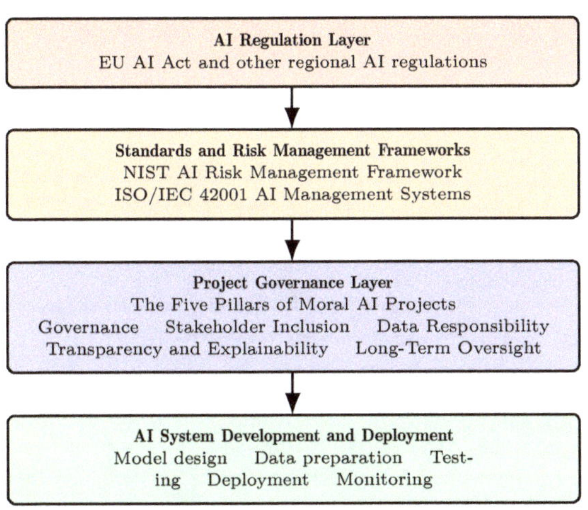

Figure 4.1: AI Frameworks of Standards and Regulations vs. Project Governance. Regulatory frameworks and technical standards define requirements for responsible AI, while the Five Pillars provide a governance structure that operationalizes these expectations within AI project leadership and delivery.

How the Five Pillars Complement Existing Frameworks

The Five Pillars serve a complementary role to existing standards and regulations.

Most external frameworks focus on either:

- **Regulatory compliance**, such as the EU AI Act, or

- **Risk management and organizational controls**, such as NIST AI RMF and ISO standards.

The Five Pillars focus specifically on *project governance*.

They translate responsible AI expectations into structures that can be embedded directly into project leadership, delivery processes, and decision checkpoints.

In practice:

- **Governance** aligns decision authority with accountability.

- **Stakeholder Inclusion** ensures affected groups are considered early in system design.

- **Data Responsibility** supports lawful, ethical, and reliable data management.

- **Transparency and Explainability** enable systems to be understood and defended.

- **Long-Term Oversight** ensures monitoring and responsibility beyond deployment.

Rather than replacing external standards, the Five Pillars help leaders apply them within the project lifecycle.

A System, Not a Checklist

The Five Pillars should not be treated as independent compliance tasks.

They operate as a governance system:

- Governance defines authority and accountability.

- Stakeholder Inclusion ensures representation and impact awareness.

- Data Responsibility protects legality, quality, and fairness.

- Transparency and Explainability make systems understandable and defensible.

- Long-Term Oversight sustains responsibility beyond deployment.

Together, they move AI projects from reactive ethics to proactive governance.

This framework does not eliminate risk.

It makes risk visible, structured, and manageable.

Governance at the Core

Governance anchors the framework.

It defines:

- Who holds decision authority

- Who carries accountability

- Who can escalate concerns

- Who must approve high-risk choices

Without governance, the other pillars weaken.

Inclusion becomes advisory. Data responsibility becomes technical. Transparency becomes optional. Oversight becomes informal.

Governance ensures that ethical commitments translate into an enforceable structure.

Operational Pillars

The remaining pillars operationalize governance across the AI lifecycle.

Stakeholder Inclusion ensures that those affected by AI systems, especially vulnerable and underrepresented groups, are considered from the outset.

Data Responsibility ensures that the data pipeline is lawful, representative, documented, and auditable.

Transparency and Explainability ensure that AI systems are understandable at appropriate levels and aligned with regulatory expectations.

Long-Term Oversight ensures that responsibility continues after deployment through monitoring, retraining, and adaptation.

Each pillar addresses a different failure pattern observed in AI projects.

Together, they form a coherent governance architecture.

Ethical Stability as an Outcome

Ethical stability is not a static state.

It results from continuous alignment between:

- Technical performance

- Legal compliance

- Stakeholder protection

- Organizational accountability

- Societal expectations

The Five Pillars create the structural conditions required to sustain this alignment.

Visualizing the Framework

The relationship between the pillars is illustrated below.

Governance anchors the system. Operational pillars extend outward. Oversight sustains ethical stability over time.

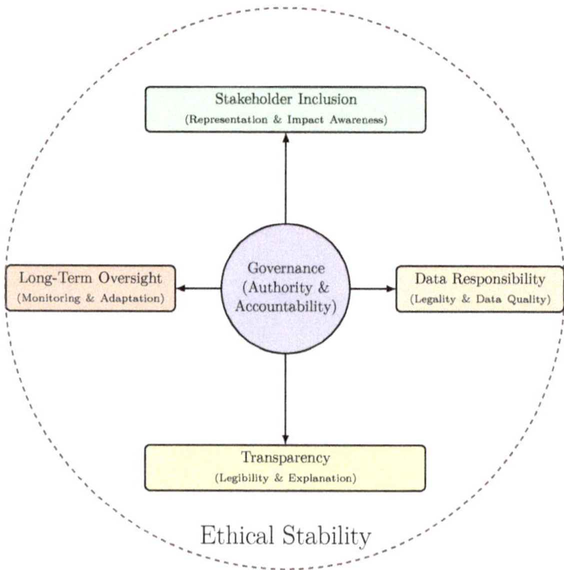

Figure 4.2: The Five Pillars of Moral AI Projects: governance anchors the system, operational pillars implement controls, and long-term oversight sustains ethical stability.

How to Use This Framework

This framework is designed for practical application.

It can be used to:

- Design new AI initiatives

- Audit existing systems

- Structure board-level reporting

- Prepare for regulatory review

- Diagnose governance weaknesses

The chapters that follow examine each pillar in detail.

They provide practical tools, structured questions, and implementation guidance.

Ethical AI is not achieved through aspiration.

It is achieved through governance discipline.

The Five Pillars provide that discipline.

Chapter 5
Pillar 1: Governance

Without governance, ethics remain an aspiration.

AI systems introduce complex decisions about data, automation, risk, and oversight. If those decisions are not structured, they default to convenience, speed, or technical preference.

Governance ensures that responsibility is deliberate rather than accidental.

AI projects therefore require more than technical coordination. They require a governance structure that makes responsibility visible, enforceable, and durable.

5.1 Why Governance Comes First

Governance Failures Are Usually Authority Failures

Many AI failures are not caused by faulty code.

They are caused by unclear authority.

When no one is explicitly responsible for approving model thresholds, reviewing ethical risks, verifying data quality, or escalating concerns, decisions are made informally.

Informal decisions weaken accountability.

Research shows that formal role definitions in AI projects often do not translate into operational accountability. Responsibilities overlap, and important duties fall between roles.

Governance closes those gaps.

These failures are not unique to AI, but AI makes them more serious. Because AI systems influence decisions about people at scale, unclear authority creates wider and faster harm.

Authority failure is the most common governance breakdown, but not the only one. The case studies in this book illustrate additional failure modes: unchecked vendor reliance, absent post-deployment monitoring, and escalation pathways that exist formally but are never used in practice. Governance must address all of these, not only the question of who holds formal authority.

Why AI Increases the Need for Governance

AI systems concentrate decision-making power in ways that are not always visible.

They operate across data, models, and automated processes that affect individuals and organizations at scale.

Without governance, these systems amplify risk:

- Decisions scale faster than oversight

- Responsibility becomes diffuse across teams

- Errors propagate across systems and stakeholders

AI project teams are moral agents. The systems they build affect real people. Governance is the structure that makes that moral responsibility operational.

5.2   What Governance Means in Practice

Governance as Clarity, Not Obstruction

Governance is not bureaucracy for its own sake.

It is the structure that enables responsible innovation.

Effective AI governance includes:

- Clearly defined decision rights

- Formal ethical review checkpoints

- Escalation routes for risk and compliance concerns

- Documented accountability assignments

- Authority to intervene when risks emerge

These mechanisms impose structure deliberately. That structure exists to protect both the people affected by the system and the organization deploying it.

Without these structures, accountability erodes under delivery pressure. With them, responsibility becomes enforceable.

Clarity alone, however, is not enough. Governance becomes real only when it shapes decision-making at key points in the project lifecycle.

From Principles to Structured Decisions

Governance becomes meaningful only when it translates into structured decision-making.

High-level commitments to fairness, transparency, or compliance are not enough. They must be embedded into how decisions are actually made.

In AI projects, governance becomes visible at key decision points:

- When models are approved

- When thresholds are set

- When deployment is authorized

- When risks are escalated

- When systems are modified or retrained

Each of these moments requires clarity about who holds authority, who carries accountability, and who can intervene.

Without that structure, governance exists only on paper.

5.3   Core Governance Mechanisms

Defining Decision Rights

This section has less vertical gap. One of the most common governance failures in AI projects is unclear decision authority.

Every AI project should explicitly define who is responsible for performing the work, who is accountable for the outcome, who must be consulted, and who must be informed. Without that clarity, accountability becomes fragmented. The governance checklist at the end of this chapter provides a practical starting point for confirming that decision authority is assigned across each critical area.

Clear decision rights reduce responsibility diffusion and strengthen governance.

Responsibility and Accountability Mapping

Decision rights identify who can decide. But governance also requires clarity about who owns the outcome of those decisions.

One practical way to make this visible is a RACI-style accountability map that records responsibility and accountability for each critical decision area.

RACI stands for *Responsible, Accountable, Consulted, and Informed.* The *Accountable* role approves the work, while the *Responsible* role performs it or ensures it is completed.

```
Decision Area        Responsible    Accountable
------------------------------------------------
Model Approval       Data Lead      Sponsor
Ethics Review        Ethics Lead    Sponsor
Deployment           Project Mgr    Sponsor
```

This structure forces clarity. It answers a critical question: who owns the decision if harm occurs?

Escalation and Intervention Authority

Governance also requires escalation pathways.

When a team member identifies unexpected bias, unacceptable error rates, data quality weaknesses, or regulatory noncompliance, there must be a clear route to elevate that concern.

Psychological safety encourages team members to speak up. But cultural willingness alone is not sufficient. Formal authority must also exist to pause, modify, or halt deployment when risks are identified. Without that authority, escalation pathways exist on paper but fail in practice.

Together, decision rights, accountability mapping, and escalation authority form the operational core of governance.

5.4 What Strong Governance Looks Like

Documentation, Sign-Off, and Audit Trails

Strong governance in AI projects means decisions are documented before implementation, ethical risks are discussed explicitly, sign-off authority is clear, and audit trails exist for key approvals.

Governance structures must also align with regulatory expectations. Under the EU AI Act, high-risk AI systems require documented risk management, conformity assessment, and audit-ready technical documentation. Organizations operating under ISO/IEC 42001-aligned management systems should embed governance checkpoints within existing quality assurance and internal audit cycles.

Governance is not about slowing innovation. It is the structure that makes innovation sustainable.

Post-Deployment Ownership

Governance does not end when deployment is approved.

Responsibility must continue after launch, when the system begins operating in the real world. Monitoring ownership must be clearly assigned. Systems must be observed, risks must be tracked, and interventions must remain possible.

Strong governance extends across the full lifecycle, not just initial approval.

5.5   Governance Readiness and Maturity

The readiness indicators in this chapter provide a practical checkpoint for project teams and sponsors. For a fuller maturity assessment, two tools are provided in the appendices. The AI Governance Readiness Scoring Model in Appendix A translates these indicators into a structured governance maturity rubric. The AI Ethical Readiness Scorecard in Appendix B provides a structured worksheet for use during governance reviews, project gates, or internal audits.

Governance Readiness Checklist

Accountability and Decision Rights

- ☐ Is a named executive sponsor formally accountable for this AI system?

- ☐ Are decision rights documented for model approval, ethics review, and deployment?

- ☐ Is a RACI-style accountability map in place for critical decision areas?

Governance Gates and Escalation

- ☐ Are approval gates defined and enforced at key life-cycle stages?

- ☐ Does ethical review precede deployment?

- ☐ Are escalation routes defined, understood, and tested in practice?

- ☐ Does formal authority exist to pause or halt deployment when risks are identified?

Documentation and Post-Deployment

- ☐ Are decisions documented with audit trails before implementation?

- ☐ Is post-deployment ownership formally assigned?

Regulatory Alignment

- ☐ Are governance structures aligned with EU AI Act and ISO/IEC 42001 requirements where applicable?

Why Governance Determines Success

AI project success depends not only on technical performance but also on the clarity of responsibility.

Governance provides the structure that makes accountability operational.

Without it, ethics remains an aspiration. With it, ethics becomes practice.

Chapter 6

Pillar 2: Stakeholder Inclusion

In traditional project governance, stakeholders are typically defined as those who influence project outcomes. In AI systems, the definition must expand to include individuals and communities who may be affected by system decisions, even if they have no direct relationship with the project.

AI systems affect far more people than direct customers. They influence individuals who never signed a contract, never attended a workshop, and never approved the system's design.

The case studies in this book illustrate what follows when those individuals are overlooked. In the facial recognition case, customers who had no awareness of the system and no power to challenge its outputs experienced direct harm. Stakeholder inclusion exists to prevent that outcome, not to remedy it after the fact.

Stakeholder inclusion ensures that those affected are considered before harm occurs, not after.

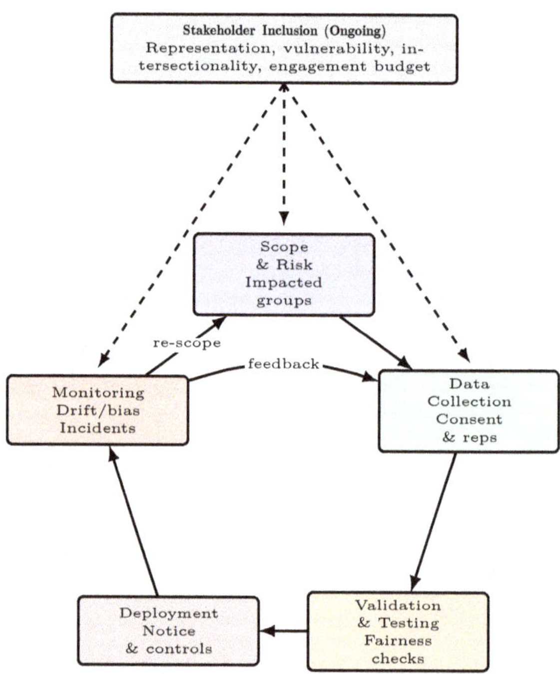

Figure 6.1: Stakeholder inclusion is continuous input to every phase. The AI project lifecycle is cyclical: monitoring feeds back into data collection and re-scoping decisions.

6.1 Why Inclusion Is a Governance Requirement

In traditional projects, stakeholder management focuses on influence. Who can fund the project? Who can block it? Who must approve it?

AI projects expand the field.

They affect individuals who may have no formal relationship with the organization, no awareness of the system, no power to challenge its outputs, and no practical ability to opt out.

Ignoring these groups does not eliminate risk. It concentrates it. Unaddressed stakeholder harm tends to surface after deployment, when design choices are costly to reverse and reputational damage is already accumulating.

Stakeholder inclusion is therefore not a public relations exercise. It is a governance discipline that must be embedded in project structures from the outset.

6.2 Stakeholder Identification and Mapping

Stakeholder inclusion begins with identifying who may be affected by the system.

At a minimum, teams should classify stakeholders by level of impact, level of influence, and degree of vulnerability or potential harm. Impact refers to the extent to which system decisions affect individuals or groups, while vulnerability reflects their ability to absorb or contest those effects.

High-impact, low-influence stakeholders require particular attention.

Research shows that many individuals affected by AI systems have limited ability to influence the project itself. These passive stakeholders may experience system outcomes without participating in the system's design, development, or deployment (Miller, 2022b).

Stakeholders Across the Lifecycle

Stakeholders appear at different points across the system lifecycle:

- **Development stakeholders**: sponsors, project managers, engineers, data scientists, and compliance teams design and build the system.

- **Operational stakeholders**: end users, operators, and system maintainers interact with or operate the system.

- **External stakeholders**: decision subjects, communities, workers, regulators, and the public are affected by its outputs.

Decision subjects are individuals whose lives, opportunities, or rights are directly shaped by system outputs; they warrant specific attention. They are frequently passive stakeholders with no influence over the project and no practical means to challenge its decisions.

Responsible AI governance expands stakeholder identification beyond influence to include potential harm.

Every project should maintain a stakeholder register that is reviewed at each major governance checkpoint. A structured stakeholder identification and inclusion tool is provided in Appendix C.

6.3 Inclusion Begins with Data

Most practitioners associate stakeholder inclusion with workshops, consultations, and advisory panels. Those mechanisms matter, but inclusion begins earlier and more fundamentally: with data.

AI systems learn from data. If certain groups are absent, underrepresented, or misrepresented in training data, the system will reflect and often amplify those gaps. This is not a technical accident. It is a structural consequence of how historical data was collected, labelled, and preserved.

Particular attention must be given to populations that are frequently underrepresented or misrepresented in historical datasets:

- Youth

- The elderly

- People with disabilities

- Economically disadvantaged groups

- Minority communities

- Intersectional populations

Intersectionality deserves specific attention. A system may perform adequately across individual demographic categories but still fail at their intersections. A model that performs well for women and well for older adults may still systematically disadvantage older women if that intersection is underrepresented in training data.

Effective inclusion at the data stage requires representative sourcing strategies, targeted outreach to underrepresented groups, bias detection across intersectional categories, and validation that includes specialized populations. Without these measures, structural blind spots become embedded in the system and are difficult to detect or correct after deployment.

This risk is examined in greater depth in the Data Responsibility chapter, where bias testing across intersectional combinations is discussed as a core data governance requirement.

6.4 Embedding Inclusion into Governance

Inclusion must be structured through governance mechanisms rather than informal consultation.

Stakeholder inclusion should be integrated into data collection planning, model validation criteria, risk assessment processes, deployment authorization gates, and post-deployment monitoring.

When inclusion is treated as a one-time activity, it fades. When embedded in governance checkpoints, it becomes operational.

Regulatory frameworks reinforce this requirement. Under the EU AI Act, high-risk AI systems must undergo fundamental rights impact assessments and demonstrate that affected populations have been considered in system design and validation. Organizations operating under ISO/IEC 42001-aligned management systems should embed stakeholder inclusion requirements within risk management processes, quality assurance checkpoints, and periodic management reviews.

6.5 Representation and Participation

Some stakeholders cannot participate directly. Children, people with severe disabilities, future users of systems not yet deployed, and communities with limited organizational access may all require representation through other means.

In such cases, representation mechanisms are necessary. These may include external advisory panels, ethics review boards, civil society consultation, independent audits, and regulatory dialogue.

Representation must be proactive rather than reactive. Proxy mechanisms must be structured and documented, not assumed.

6.6 Resourcing Inclusion

Meaningful inclusion requires resources.

Organizations often express commitment to stakeholder engagement but allocate no dedicated budget and assign no accountable owner. Without funding and ownership, inclusion becomes symbolic.

Budget should be allocated for stakeholder workshops and consultations, outreach to underrepresented groups, data collection in diverse communities, accessibility accommodations, independent impact assessments, and communication and transparency initiatives.

Each inclusion activity should have a named accountable owner. Budget without ownership is as weak as no budget at all.

6.7 Stakeholder Inclusion Readiness

The following quick diagnostic can be used during governance reviews, project gates, or internal audits. It is independent of the detailed scoring rubric in Appendix A and the structured scorecard in Appendix B, which provide fuller maturity assessments across all five pillars.

A more detailed stakeholder identification and inclusion process, including a structured register and representation planning tool, is provided in Appendix C.

Stakeholder Inclusion Readiness Checklist

Identification and Mapping

☐ Are development, operational, and external stakeholders identified?

☐ Are passive stakeholders explicitly identified and documented?

☐ Are decision subjects identified as a distinct group requiring specific attention?

☐ Has potential harm been assessed alongside power, legitimacy, and urgency?

☐ Is a stakeholder register maintained and reviewed at each governance checkpoint?

Representation and Participation

☐ Are representation mechanisms defined for low-voice and hard-to-reach groups?

☐ Does data collection strategy address representation gaps and intersectional bias?

☐ Is validation testing conducted across intersectional population groups?

Continued

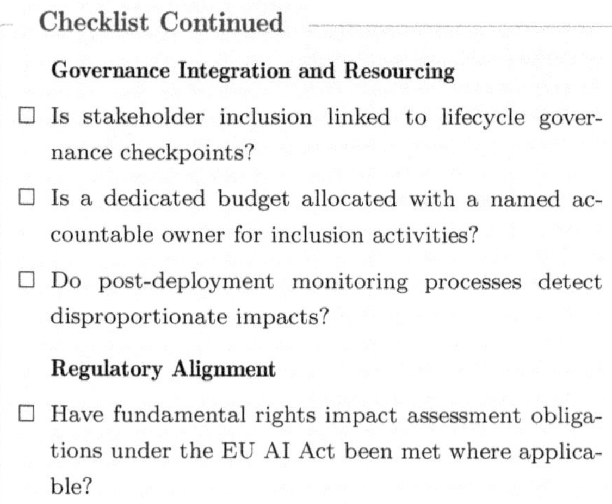

Checklist Continued

Governance Integration and Resourcing

☐ Is stakeholder inclusion linked to lifecycle governance checkpoints?

☐ Is a dedicated budget allocated with a named accountable owner for inclusion activities?

☐ Do post-deployment monitoring processes detect disproportionate impacts?

Regulatory Alignment

☐ Have fundamental rights impact assessment obligations under the EU AI Act been met where applicable?

Why Inclusion Defines Responsible AI

AI systems do not fail because stakeholders are complex.

They fail because stakeholders are invisible.

Responsible AI governance makes those stakeholders visible early, before design choices become difficult or costly to change.

Inclusion is not an optional enhancement.

It is a structural requirement for responsible AI projects.

Chapter 7

Pillar 3: Data Responsibility

Data shapes outcomes.

AI systems do not invent their own logic; they learn patterns from the data provided.

If the data is incomplete, biased, unlawfully obtained, poorly documented, or misaligned with purpose, the system will reflect those weaknesses.

Data responsibility is therefore both a technical requirement and a governance obligation.

It is the foundation of trustworthy AI.

If governance fails at the data level, no amount of model tuning can fully repair the harm.

The copyright case in this book illustrates one dimension of that failure.

- Models were trained on copyrighted material without appropriate licensing.

- The data pipeline had not been treated as a controlled process.

The facial recognition case illustrates another.

- Underrepresentation in training data resulted in a system that performed poorly for certain groups,

- The result was direct harm to individuals who were unaware of or had no influence over the system that affected them.

Data responsibility exists to prevent both kinds of failure.

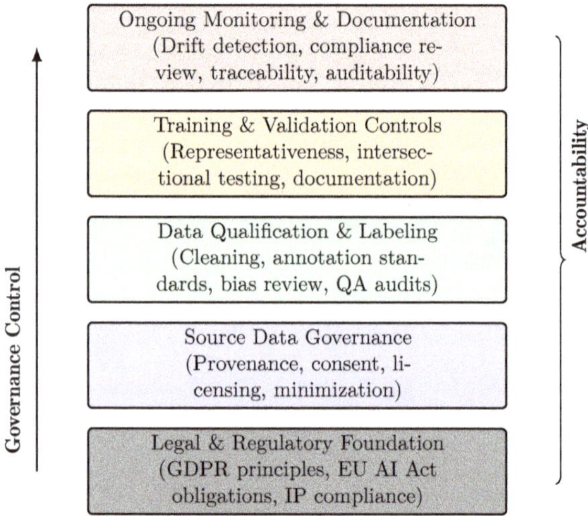

Figure 7.1: Data Governance Stack: layered controls supported by governance control and end-to-end accountability.

7.1　The Data Pipeline and Its Risks

Why Data Is a Governance Issue

Many AI harms originate not in the model architecture but in the data pipeline.

Data responsibility begins long before model training. It covers how source data is collected, cleaned and labeled, transformed into training datasets, documented and stored, and monitored over time.

Organizations often treat data as an asset.

Under European regulatory frameworks, it is also a liability. Organizations that cannot demonstrate lawful sourcing, purpose alignment, and bias controls face regulatory penalties, legal disputes, and reputational harm.

Data responsibility is best managed as a stack of practical controls:

- **Lawful sourcing**: clear provenance, legal basis, and consent or licensing where required

- **Purpose alignment**: data use constrained to defined purpose, with controls against purpose creep

- **Data quality**: cleaning, normalization, de-duplication, accuracy checks, and completeness review

- **Representativeness**: subgroup and intersectional coverage, with documented bias testing

- **Documentation**: traceability records, audit logs, and compliance evidence

- **Supply chain control**: vendor governance for third-party data, labeling, and transfers

- **Change control**: governance for dataset updates and retraining inputs

The sections that follow provide practical guidance for each area.

Source Data vs. Training Data

It is important to distinguish between two stages of the data pipeline.

Source Data is the raw data collected from individuals, devices, systems, or third parties.

Training Data is the curated, processed, and labeled dataset used to train AI models.

Risk exists at both levels.

Source data may involve:

- Unclear consent

- Secondary use beyond original purpose

- Excessive data collection

- Sensitive personal information

- Data acquired from opaque third-party vendors

Training data introduces additional risks:

- Selection bias

- Labeling bias

- Underrepresentation of minority or intersectional groups

- Data leakage

- Improper feature engineering

Responsible AI projects treat the data pipeline as a controlled process at both stages.

7.2   Representativeness, Bias, and Judgment

Understanding the data pipeline explains where risks arise.

The next question is how those risks shape outcomes, particularly through representativeness and bias.

Representativeness as a Value Judgment

When political polls ask a group of people for their opinions and report those results as public opinion, they rely on a subset to represent a whole population. AI systems work the same way.

Datasets stand in for reality. But this relationship is never neutral.

A dataset reflects choices about what counts, who is visible, and which differences are measured (Chasalow & Levy, 2021).

When project teams decide who is included or excluded from source data, they determine which people and experiences the system can recognize. Those decisions affect both model performance and ethical outcomes.

Representativeness is therefore a value judgment, not only a technical property.

A dataset may be inexpensive to obtain because it excludes people who are harder to reach, less visible, or more costly to include. That does not make it responsibly representative. It may only make it convenient.

The data responsibility checklist at the end of this chapter provides a set of governance questions teams should ask before treating any dataset as fit for purpose.

When More Data Is Not Better

Larger datasets do not automatically produce fairer or more reliable systems.

If additional data repeat existing bias, add noise, or expand surveillance without improving representation, it can increase harm rather than reduce it.

Larger datasets also increase:

- Data management complexity

- Labeling and annotation effort

- Storage and security exposure

- Governance and audit requirements

Training large AI models requires substantial computing power, energy, and infrastructure, including electricity, cooling, and water (Bender et al., 2021). These costs scale with dataset and model size.

Projects should justify increases in data volume based on measurable improvements in fairness, accuracy, or safety.

- Expanded collection may lead to excessive tracking, intrusive monitoring, or disproportionate burden on certain groups.

- Increasing visibility creates new exposure.

Responsible teams must decide when more data is necessary, when less data is safer, and when alternative approaches including synthetic or aggregated data are more appropriate than expanding collection.

Data does not simply reflect the world. It is shaped by how we define, measure, and record it, and these choices can reinforce the patterns they aim to describe.

Representativeness is a trade-off between accuracy, fairness, cost, burden, and human dignity.

Better governed data is more valuable than more data.

To support practical application, Appendix D provides a structured checklist for evaluating whether data collection is responsible, proportionate, and justified.

Historical Bias and Structural Inequality

Representativeness is closely linked to historical bias.

Even well-constructed datasets may reproduce inequality if the underlying data reflects past decisions made under conditions of discrimination or exclusion.

AI systems learn from historical patterns.

If those patterns reflected inequality, the system will reproduce them at scale and apply them to decision subjects who have no awareness of the data that shaped their outcomes.

Common data-related risks include:

- Historical bias embedded in legacy records

- Underrepresentation of vulnerable populations

- Proxy variables that indirectly encode protected characteristics

- Skewed outcome labels based on subjective human judgment

Bias is not always visible in aggregate statistics. It often appears at subgroup or intersectional levels.

Intersectionality deserves particular attention.

A system may perform adequately across individual demographic categories but still fail at their intersections.

A model that performs well for women and well for older adults may still systematically disadvantage older women if that specific intersection is underrepresented in training data.

The same pattern can appear across any combination of characteristics: race and disability, income and geography, age and language.

Aggregate performance metrics can hide these failures entirely.

A system that is 94 percent accurate overall may still be consistently wrong for a specific subgroup that makes up a small share of the test data. For the individuals in that group, the overall accuracy figure is meaningless.

Responsible teams do not rely on aggregate metrics alone.

They test explicitly across subgroup and intersectional combinations before deployment and document the results.

7.3　Regulatory and Legal Foundations

Regulatory Foundations: GDPR

The General Data Protection Regulation (GDPR) is a European Union law governing how organizations collect, use, and protect personal data (European Commission, 2016).

It gives individuals rights over their data and requires organizations to handle personal information transparently, securely, and responsibly.

It is referenced here because it represents one of the most comprehensive and influential approaches to governing personal data. Similar frameworks have been adopted in other regions and several US states.

Under the GDPR, personal data processing must comply with seven core principles:

- Lawfulness, fairness, and transparency

- Purpose limitation

- Data minimization

- Accuracy

- Storage limitation

- Integrity and confidentiality

- Accountability

For AI projects, this means:

- Establishing a clear legal basis for data processing

- Explicitly defining the purpose before model training

- Avoiding excessive data collection

- Maintaining mechanisms to correct inaccurate data

- Applying security safeguards throughout the data lifecycle

- Producing documentation demonstrating compliance

Where automated decision-making produces legal or similarly significant effects on individuals, GDPR's right to explanation is engaged. Individuals may request meaningful information about the logic involved and contest the outcome.

Data responsibility must therefore be aligned with individual rights, not only technical performance.

Risk-Based Obligations: EU AI Act

The EU AI Act establishes a risk-based governance regime for AI systems (European Union, 2024). It classifies systems according to their level of risk and imposes stronger requirements on those that could significantly affect people's rights, safety, or opportunities.

For high-risk AI systems, data obligations include:

- Maintaining high-quality training, validation, and testing datasets

- Applying appropriate data governance and management practices

- Documenting data characteristics and limitations

- Implementing bias mitigation procedures

- Producing technical documentation sufficient for regulatory review

Projects delivering systems in regulated sectors such as healthcare, finance, employment, or public services must ensure that dataset quality is demonstrable rather than assumed.

Data responsibility is now legally auditable.

Intellectual Property and Copyright Risk

AI systems increasingly rely on large datasets of text, images, audio, video, and code.

Not all of this data is legally usable.

Training models on copyrighted material without appropriate licensing or legal basis may expose organizations to:

- Copyright infringement claims

- Breach of licensing agreements

- Contractual liability

- Regulatory scrutiny

- Reputational damage

The legal status of training on copyrighted content remains an evolving area across jurisdictions.

Organizations must assess:

- Whether training data includes copyrighted works

- Whether licenses explicitly permit model training

- Whether text and data mining exceptions apply

- Whether opt-out mechanisms have been respected

- Whether internal policies align with applicable IP law

Under European law, documentation and traceability of data sources are increasingly important.

If data provenance cannot be demonstrated, governance risk increases.

Responsible AI projects treat intellectual property review as part of data governance, not as an afterthought.

Personal Agency and Weak Governance Contexts

Regulatory frameworks set minimum expectations. However, in some environments, laws and enforcement are weak, unclear, or applied inconsistently.

In these contexts, organizations may assume that broad data collection is acceptable because it is legal or unlikely to be challenged. This assumption is flawed.

- Legal permission does not mean ethical legitimacy.

- Weak governance does not remove personal agency.

- People remain moral subjects even when institutions fail to protect them.

This is most important where individuals have limited ability to refuse data collection, understand how their data is used, or challenge outcomes that affect them.

In these situations:

- Opt-out options may be unrealistic or inaccessible.

- Individuals may not understand how their data is used.

- Harmful outcomes may be difficult to challenge.

- Systems may be deployed before safeguards are in place.

For responsible AI projects, data responsibility cannot stop at legal compliance. Teams must consider whether affected individuals retain meaningful agency.

Where institutional protections are limited, governance must be stronger.

The absence of strong law is not permission. It is a signal to act with greater care.

To support practical application, Appendix D provides a structured checklist for assessing whether data collection respects personal agency, especially in weak governance environments.

7.4   Operational Controls for Responsible Data

Regulatory frameworks define expectations. Operational controls determine whether those expectations are met in practice.

Data Supply Chain Responsibility

AI systems frequently rely on third-party data providers, annotation services, or external model components.

Responsibility does not end at procurement.

Organizations must assess

- Vendor data sourcing practices

- Consent and licensing validity

- Annotation workforce conditions

- Security standards

- Data transfer mechanisms across jurisdictions

Data supply chains can introduce hidden risk.

If provenance cannot be traced, governance is weakened.

Traceability and documentation are core elements of responsible AI.

Data Minimization vs. Model Performance

A common tension exists between collecting more data to improve model accuracy and limiting data collection to comply with privacy principles.

Responsible AI projects:

- Define purpose clearly before expanding datasets

- Justify each category of personal data collected

- Avoid collecting sensitive attributes without legal and ethical necessity

- Evaluate whether synthetic or aggregated data can reduce privacy risk without compromising model quality

More data may mean greater liability but not necessarily better outcomes.

The Hidden Cost of Data Qualification

High-quality AI systems require qualified data. Qualification takes time.

Before training begins, data must be:

- Cleaned

- Normalized

- De-duplicated

- Anonymized or pseudonymized where required

- Reviewed for representativeness

- Assessed for bias

Organizations frequently underestimate the time and cost required to transform raw data into compliant, usable training data.

Shortcuts at this stage create long-term risk.

Labeling and Annotation Responsibility

Many AI systems depend on labeled data.

Labeling is the process of adding meaningful tags or categories to raw data so that an AI model can learn from it.

A human reviewer might look at a photograph and mark it as "pedestrian" or "vehicle" for a self-driving car system, or read a customer complaint and classify it as "billing issue" or "technical fault" for a support routing system. Those labels become the ground truth the model trains on. If the labels are inconsistent, culturally biased, or poorly defined, the model will learn and reproduce those errors at scale.

Annotation processes are often outsourced to third-party platforms.

This introduces further concerns about:

- Worker conditions

- Data security

- Cultural bias in labeling

- Inconsistent category interpretation.

Labeling is not neutral.

It embeds human judgment into the dataset, and those judgments shape model behavior.

Responsible AI projects document labeling standards and conduct periodic quality audits.

Time, Cost, and Realistic Planning

Data responsibility requires investment.

It extends project timelines and increases upfront costs.

However, insufficient qualification increases downstream costs through:

- Model retraining

- Compliance remediation

- Legal disputes

- Reputational damage

- Regulatory penalties

Project planning must therefore include:

- Dedicated time for dataset qualification

- Budget for annotation and review

- Legal review of data licensing and intellectual property

- Technical validation cycles

- Independent fairness testing where required

If the project schedule does not include time for data qualification, the plan is unrealistic.

If the budget does not include resources for proper labeling and review, data governance will be compromised.

7.5 Sustaining Data Responsibility in Practice

Implementing controls is not sufficient.

Data responsibility must be sustained over time through monitoring, documentation, and continuous review.

Documentation and Auditability

Data responsibility must be documented.

This includes

- Dataset provenance records

- Data preprocessing logs

- Bias testing documentation

- Fairness evaluation results

- Data protection impact assessments where required

The Dataset Governance Assessment checklist in Appendix D and the Dataset Governance and Model Card worksheets in Appendix E provide structured tools for working through these decisions and recording the evidence in a form that is audit-ready and traceable.

Used together, they document both the data the system was built on and how the model behaves when using it, making those decisions visible to auditors, reviewers, and regulators.

Documentation serves three purposes: internal accountability, regulatory defensibility, and continuous improvement. If dataset decisions are undocumented, they cannot be reviewed, challenged, or improved.

Data Responsibility Readiness

For a detailed maturity assessment, the AI Governance Readiness Scoring Model in Appendix A and the AI Ethical Readiness Scorecard in Appendix B provide structured tools for evaluating data responsibility governance across the project lifecycle.

Data responsibility does not end at deployment. Choices about data sourcing, representation, labeling, and documentation shape how the system behaves in the real world and determine whether it can be monitored, updated, and governed responsibly over time. These links to post-deployment governance are discussed in Chapter 9.

Data Responsibility Readiness Checklist

Lawful Sourcing and Purpose

☐ Is the legal basis for data collection and processing documented?

☐ Is data use constrained to its defined purpose, with controls against purpose creep?

☐ Are source data and training data distinguished and governed separately?

Continued

Checklist Continued

Representativeness and Bias

☐ Has representativeness been assessed, including subgroup and intersectional coverage?

☐ How was the data collected, and who may be missing because they were difficult or costly to include?

☐ Would collecting more data require exploitation, coercion, or surveillance?

☐ Are bias testing methods documented and repeatable across intersectional groups?

Annotation, Qualification, and Documentation

☐ Are annotation and labeling standards documented with quality controls in place?

☐ Does the project plan include dedicated time and budget for data qualification?

☐ Are dataset provenance records and preprocessing logs maintained?

☐ Has a model card been completed and made available to non-technical reviewers?

Continued

> ### Checklist Continued
>
> **Legal and Intellectual Property**
>
> ☐ Have third-party data licensing and intellectual property obligations been verified?
>
> ☐ Has a data protection impact assessment been conducted where required?
>
> **Personal Agency and Governance Context**
>
> ☐ Do affected individuals retain meaningful agency over how their data is collected?
>
> ☐ Do affected individuals retain meaningful agency over how their data is used?
>
> ☐ Where governance environments are weak, have stronger internal controls been applied?

Why Data Responsibility Defines Ethical AI

AI systems inherit the strengths and weaknesses of their data.

Responsible data practices reduce bias, protect individual rights, strengthen regulatory compliance, and improve long-term system reliability.

Data responsibility is the foundation of trustworthy AI.

If governance fails at the data level, no amount of model tuning can fully repair the harm.

Chapter 8

Pillar 4: Transparency and Explainability

When an AI system makes a decision that affects someone, that person deserves to know what happened and why.

Without transparency, decisions cannot be reviewed or challenged.

Without explainability, the people affected by a system have no real way to question its outputs or hold anyone accountable.

The generative AI misuse case in this book shows what happens when these conditions are missing.

- A professional submitted legal documents containing citations that did not exist.

- The AI system had produced them confidently, without any warning that it might be wrong.

- The system's limits were invisible to the person relying on it.

Transparency and explainability are designed to prevent exactly that kind of failure.

Together, they make AI systems governable.

8.1 Why Transparency Is a Governance Requirement

AI systems use data, models, and logic that most people never see.

When that logic is hidden, decisions cannot be reviewed, risks are harder to spot early, accountability is harder to enforce, and individuals cannot challenge outcomes that affect them.

Transparency is not simply about good communication. It is a governance requirement that keeps responsibility visible and enforceable throughout the life of the system.

When transparency is missing, trust breaks down. When it is present and meaningful, it becomes the foundation for accountability.

8.2 Risks of Opaque Systems

Before looking at what transparency requires, it helps to be clear about what its absence produces.

Systems that operate without transparency tend to:

- Cause loss of trust among users and the people affected

- Resistance to using or overseeing the system

- Regulatory investigation and possible penalties

- Legal disputes where the system's logic cannot be reconstructed

- Confusion inside the organization about who is responsible

Opacity does not make a system simpler. It hides complexity, so problems go undetected until they cause harm.

Transparency makes complexity manageable.

8.3 Transparency as a Multi-Layered System

Transparency is not a single document or disclosure. It works at several levels, each serving a different audience:

1. Internal technical documentation
2. Client or sponsor-level explanation
3. User-level explanation
4. Public or regulatory disclosure where required

Mixing up these levels leads to two common problems:

- giving non-technical audiences more technical detail than they can use, and

- giving the people most affected by the system too little information to understand what happened.

Transparency by Audience

The table below sets out the minimum disclosure requirements for each audience. Each level is a floor, not a ceiling.

```
Audience           Minimum disclosure requirements
-------------------------------------------------
Internal teams     Model purpose; data sources;
                   metrics; bias tests;
                   limitations; change logs.

Client/Sponsor     Intended use; risk boundaries;
                   key metrics; constraints;
                   governance owner.

Users              Clear notice that AI is used;
                   what it does;
                   why it made a decision;
                   how to challenge it;
                   what limitations apply.

Public             System category;
   /Regulator      documentation access;
                   required disclosures;
                   incident reporting.
```

This structure ensures that transparency is meaningful rather
than symbolic.

8.4　Core Transparency Mechanisms

Internal Technical Transparency

Inside the project team, transparency means keeping thorough records.

These records should cover:

- Why the model was built the way it was

- Where the training data came from

- Which features were used and why

- How well the system performs

- What the system cannot do or does poorly

- The results of bias testing

- How the system was validated

One practical tool for capturing this information is a model card (Mitchell et al., 2019).

A model card is a short, structured document that describes:

- What a model does

- How well it performs

- Where it falls short

- What it should not be used for

It is written so that both technical and non-technical reviewers can understand it.

Model cards support audits, accountability reviews, and regulatory inspections.

A model card template is provided in Appendix E. It is designed for use across stakeholder groups, not only engineering teams, and covers the transparency obligations most relevant to governance reviews and pre-deployment sign-off. It also sets out who is responsible for preparing, reviewing, and maintaining the card across the system lifecycle.

Without solid internal documentation, governance breaks down regardless of what is communicated to users or regulators.

Model Interpretability and Design Trade-offs

How transparent a system can be depends partly on how it was designed. Some models are easier to interpret than others. Models that prioritize high performance often do so by becoming more complex, which makes it harder to explain what they are doing and why.

Two properties matter most for governance:

- **Robustness**: the system produces consistent results across different inputs and conditions.

- **Traceability**: it is possible to trace a specific output back to the inputs that produced it.

When a model is hard to interpret, additional explanation tools must be built around it.

Choosing a model architecture is therefore a governance decision, not just a technical one.

Explainability by Audience

Explanations must suit the person receiving them.

For clients and sponsors, an explanation should cover:

- What the system is designed to do

- How well it performs

- Where its limits are

- What risks it carries

- Who is responsible for it

For users and decision subjects an explanation should answer:

- why this decision was made

- what information influenced the outcome

- whether the decision can be challenged

- what the system cannot reliably do

Some organizations resist providing explanations because they worry about exposing proprietary methods. That concern is understandable but usually overstated.

Explainability does not mean sharing model architecture or trade secrets. It means giving people a clear, honest account of what happened and why.

User Interface Transparency

Transparency must be visible to users when they interact with the system, not only in background documentation.

Even a well-documented system can feel opaque if the interface:

- Hides what inputs were used

- Shows outputs without any context

- Uses language that is hard to understand

- Does not communicate how confident the system is

Good interface design should:

- Clearly tell users that AI is involved

- Show confidence levels where relevant

- Offer plain-language explanations of outputs

- Avoid misleading visualizations

- Make it clear whether an output is a recommendation or a binding decision

A common failure is presenting probabilistic output as a definitive answer. A confidence score of 73 percent, shown without explanation, can easily be read as a reliable verdict rather than an uncertain estimate.

When that happens, the interface undermines transparency rather than supports it.

To support practical application, Appendix E provides a User Interface Synopsis worksheet to assess whether a user interface clearly communicates purpose, limitations, risks, and accountability before it is deployed to real users.

Communicating Uncertainty and Limitations

Every AI system has limits.

Being transparent means stating clearly:

- What the system is designed to do

- What it is not designed to do

- Where it works well

- Where it is likely to fail or perform poorly

Staying silent about limitations increases both ethical and legal risk. It also removes the information that people need to oversee the system effectively.

8.5   Regulatory Transparency Requirements

Transparency is now a legal requirement in many contexts, not just a good practice.

Under GDPR, individuals have a right to explanation when automated systems make decisions that significantly affect them.

Organizations must:

- Provide meaningful information about the logic involved in the decision

- Give individuals a way to contest the outcome

- Enable individuals to request human review or intervention in the decision

The EU AI Act adds further requirements for high-risk systems.

- Users must be informed when interacting with certain AI systems.

- Instructions for use must describe purpose, capabilities, limitations, and risks.

- System operation must be traceable through logging and documentation.

- Technical documentation must support conformity assessment prior to deployment.

The EU AI Act also requires that AI-generated content be clearly labeled.

If a system produces text, images, audio, or video, users must be told that AI created it. This prevents people from being misled about where the content came from.

Transparency is no longer optional. It is a legal obligation.

8.6   Transparency Readiness

For a fuller assessment, the AI Governance Readiness Scoring Model in Appendix A and the AI Ethical Readiness Scorecard in Appendix B provide structured tools for evaluating transparency governance across the project lifecycle.

Appendix E provides structured worksheets for documenting the dataset, model, user interface, and oversight arrangements in a form that supports audit, regulatory review, and stakeholder accountability.

Transparency Readiness Checklist

Internal Documentation

☐ Is technical documentation complete, audit-ready, and accessible to non-technical reviewers?

☐ Has a model card been completed and made available for reviews and pre-deployment sign-off?

☐ Are performance metrics, limitations, and bias testing results clearly recorded?

☐ Has the choice of model architecture been assessed as a governance decision, not only a technical one?

Continued

Checklist Continued

Audience-Specific Transparency

☐ Is audience-specific transparency provided for internal teams, clients, users, and regulators?

☐ Do users receive a clear notice that AI is involved and an explanation of what it does?

☐ Are users told why a decision was made and how they can challenge it?

☐ Are decision challenge mechanisms available and accessible to affected individuals?

Interface and Communication

☐ Does the interface communicate confidence levels and distinguish recommendations from binding decisions?

☐ Are system limitations and uncertainty communicated clearly at the point of use?

Regulatory Alignment

☐ Is AI-generated content labeled as required under the EU AI Act?

☐ Are GDPR right to explanation obligations met for automated decisions that significantly affect individuals?

Why Transparency Defines Trust

People cannot trust a system they cannot understand.

They cannot challenge a decision they cannot see.

And they cannot be held accountable for outcomes they had no way to scrutinize.

Transparency and explainability are not add-ons.

They are what make it possible for AI systems to be used responsibly, overseen effectively, and trusted by the people they affect.

Chapter 9

Pillar 5: Long-Term Oversight

Deployment is not the finish line.

It is the point at which a system begins to affect real people under real conditions that no project team can fully predict in advance.

The automated trading case in this book shows what happens when that reality is ignored.

- A system designed to manage risk automatically triggered a cascade of liquidations, causing serious financial harm to investors.

- There was no structured post-deployment monitoring to detect the problem before it compounded.

- By the time the failure was visible, the damage was done.

The auto loan algorithm case shows that the same failure can occur quietly, without any single dramatic event.

- Systematic errors in loan calculations affected dealerships and borrowers across many transactions.

- The system's logic could not be traced back to its inputs, there was no monitoring to catch the problem earlier, and no documentation to support audit or review.

- Errors accumulated quietly until the damage was already done.

Long-term oversight exists to catch both kinds of failure, the sudden and the slow, and to ensure that the people responsible for a system remain accountable for it long after it goes live.

9.1   Why Long-Term Oversight Matters

Many AI harms do not appear immediately.

They emerge gradually through:

- Model drift as real-world data diverges from training data

- Changes in user behavior that the system was not designed for

- Unanticipated use cases that push the system beyond its intended scope

- Evolving regulatory requirements that change what is permissible

A system that performed well at deployment may degrade months later without anyone noticing.

As systems become more automated, human touchpoints decrease.

- The natural moments that once prompted review, such as a decision that surprised someone or a result that was questioned, occur less often.

- Higher automation does not guarantee stronger accountability.

- Without deliberate monitoring, accountability weakens as the system becomes more embedded and more complex.

Long-term oversight ensures that systems remain aligned with legal, ethical, and organizational standards after deployment, not just at launch.

9.2 Core Oversight Mechanisms

Continuous Monitoring

Long-term oversight requires measurable, scheduled monitoring.

This includes:

- Accuracy tracking over time

- False positive and false negative monitoring

- Bias detection across demographic and intersectional groups

- Performance comparison against baseline metrics

- Monitoring for data drift

Monitoring should not be reactive. It should be planned, scheduled, and documented before deployment begins.

Under the EU AI Act, providers of high-risk systems must establish post-market monitoring systems capable of collecting, documenting, and analyzing performance data throughout the system's lifecycle.

Monitoring Cadence

Monitoring cadence defines how often different aspects of an AI system are reviewed and what is evaluated at each interval.

It translates oversight from an abstract requirement into a structured, repeatable practice.

A well-defined rhythm of reviews ensures that monitoring is proportionate to risk, aligned with system behavior, and sustained over time.

It also creates predictability.

Teams know when reviews occur, what evidence must be collected, and who is responsible for evaluation and escalation.

Monitoring activities operate across different time horizons.

- Frequent reviews focus on operational signals that indicate immediate risk or system instability.

- Periodic reviews assess performance, fairness, and compliance over time.

```
Frequency        What to review
-------------------------------------------------------
Daily/Weekly     Alerts: error spikes,
                 drift signals,
                 incident reports,
                 unusual usage patterns.
Monthly          Performance: accuracy,
                 false positives/negatives,
                 subgroup bias metrics,
                 overrides.
Quarterly        Governance: compliance review,
                 retention/minimization checks,
                 access controls,
                 vendor changes,
                 documentation updates.
Biannual/        Impact review: security posture,
                 stakeholder harm signals,
Annual           benefits vs protections,
                 retraining strategy,
                 audit readiness.
Event-based      Triggered by: retraining,
                 major data changes,
                 new use cases,
                 complaint trends,
                 serious incidents,
                 regulatory changes.
```

- Longer-cycle reviews evaluate broader impact, strategic alignment, and emerging risks.

- Event-based reviews ensure that significant changes or incidents trigger immediate reassessment rather than waiting for the next scheduled cycle.

Cadence turns oversight into a routine practice rather than an emergency response.

Retraining Governance

AI systems are frequently retrained as new data becomes available or as performance degrades.

Each retraining cycle introduces new risk.

The updated model may use new data that changes how it behaves, shifts its bias patterns, or affects how well it works for specific groups.

Sometimes, synthetic or aggregated data is used to fill representation gaps identified during monitoring. That approach can help, but it requires its own governance controls to ensure the synthetic data does not create new problems.

Retraining must be governed as a formal change process. It should include re-validation of dataset quality, updated bias testing, documentation of model changes, re-approval by accountable roles, and review of regulatory classification where relevant.

When retraining occurs, the model card in Appendix E must be updated to reflect the new data sources, revised performance metrics, and any changes to known limitations or validated populations.

An outdated model card after retraining is a governance gap.

Usage Controls and Human Oversight

Oversight includes how the system is used, not just how it performs.

Organizations must define:

- Who may access the system

- Under what conditions it may be used

- When human review is required

- How overrides are handled and documented

- How misuse is detected

Usage controls prevent systems from being applied beyond their intended scope.

Under the EU AI Act, human oversight mechanisms must be designed so that users can effectively interpret outputs and intervene when needed.

But as Chapter 17 discusses, effective human oversight is not only a procedural matter.

It is a cultural one.

Humans can be formally in the loop while being practically discouraged from intervening.

Oversight mechanisms must therefore be supported by a leadership culture that treats intervention as expected rather than as a sign of system failure.

Incident Reporting and Escalation

Oversight mechanisms must include:

- Internal reporting channels

- Defined escalation thresholds

- Incident documentation

- Regulatory notification where required

The EU AI Act requires reporting of serious incidents and malfunctions for high-risk systems.

The regulatory and reputational consequences of an undocumented incident are significantly worse than those of a well-managed one.

9.3 Governance Over Time

Long-term oversight is not a single control or periodic check. It is a structured set of governance activities that evolve over time as systems operate, data changes, and impacts emerge.

Figure 9.1 should be read as a governance-over-time map. It links key areas of review to the points in time when they must be actively governed.

Rather than depicting monitoring alone, it shows how responsibility shifts and expands across the system lifecycle, connecting operational oversight to data governance, organizational accountability, and strategic decision-making.

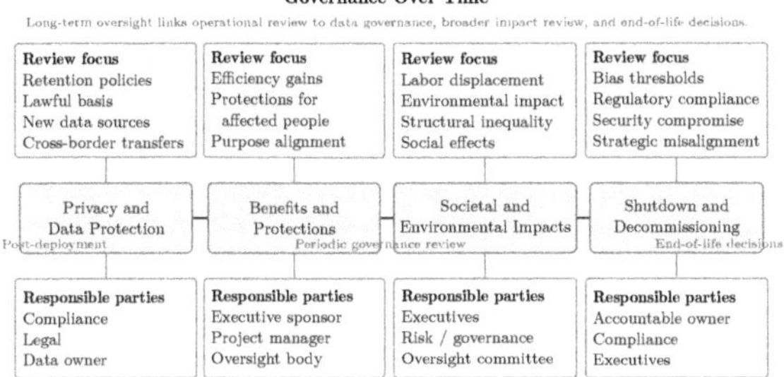

Figure 9.1: Illustrative governance-over-time timeline showing the main review areas, governance focus, and responsible parties after deployment.

Privacy and Data Protection Over Time

Data protection obligations do not end at deployment.

Under GDPR, organizations must ensure:

- Continued lawfulness of processing,

- Data minimization,

- Storage limitation,

- Security safeguards, and

- Respect for data subject rights throughout the system's life.

Long-term oversight includes

- Periodic review of retention policies

- Validation that new data sources remain compliant

- Reassessment of lawful basis when use cases expand

- Review of cross-border data transfers

Data collected for one purpose must not quietly expand into unrelated uses.

Purpose creep is one of the most common sources of compliance risk in operational AI systems.

When monitoring reveals that data use has drifted from its original purpose, or that new data sources are needed to address representation gaps, the data responsibility controls described in Chapter 7 must be revisited.

Monitoring outcomes and data governance are not separate concerns. They are connected across the full system lifecycle.

Benefits and Protections in Balance

AI systems often promise efficiency, cost reduction, or improved prediction.

Long-term oversight must evaluate whether those benefits remain aligned with protections for the people the system affects.

The oversight checklist at the end of this chapter includes questions that help teams assess whether that balance is being maintained.

Efficiency alone is not a sufficient measure of success.

Societal and Environmental Impacts

AI systems can have consequences that extend well beyond individual decisions.

These include:

- Labor displacement in affected industries

- Environmental impact from ongoing energy consumption

- Reinforcement of structural inequality over time

- Social polarization driven by automated content or recommendation systems

- Market distortion from algorithmic pricing or trading

Long-term oversight includes a periodic review of these broader impacts.

Ethical maturity means looking beyond immediate performance metrics to the wider effects a system produces over time.

Shutdown and Decommissioning

Every AI system should have defined shutdown criteria established before deployment.

These may include:

- Persistent bias beyond acceptable thresholds

- Regulatory non-compliance

- Security compromise

- Strategic misalignment with organizational purpose

- Demonstrated societal harm

Decommissioning should include:

- Data retention review in line with legal obligations

- User notification where necessary

- Archiving of documentation, including the model card

- Structured evaluation of lessons learned

Responsible AI includes knowing when to stop.

9.4   Oversight Maturity and Readiness

Strong oversight is structured, documented, and continuous.

It does not rely on individuals remembering to check.

It is built into project roles, governance cycles, and organizational routines, ensuring it happens regardless of staff changes, delivery pressure, or competing priorities.

Appendix E provides a one-page worksheet to document the long-term oversight requirements for monitoring, governing, and, if necessary, decommissioning an AI system after deployment.

For a comprehensive maturity assessment, the AI Governance Readiness Scoring Model in Appendix A and the AI Ethical Readiness Scorecard in Appendix B provide structured tools to evaluate long-term oversight and governance throughout the project lifecycle.

Long-Term Oversight Readiness Checklist

Continuous Monitoring

☐ Is a post-market monitoring plan documented and active before deployment?

☐ Is monitoring scheduled at defined intervals covering accuracy, bias, and drift?

☐ Are false positive and false negative rates tracked across demographic and intersectional groups?

☐ Are performance results compared against baseline metrics on a regular schedule?

Retraining Governance

☐ Is retraining governed as a formal change process with re-validation and re-approval?

☐ Is the model card updated each time the model is retrained?

Continued

Checklist Continued

Usage Controls and Human Oversight

☐ Are usage controls defined, including access permissions and override procedures?

☐ Do human oversight mechanisms allow users to effectively interpret and intervene in outputs?

Incident Reporting

☐ Are internal incident reporting channels active with defined escalation thresholds?

☐ Are serious incident reporting obligations under the EU AI Act understood and met?

Privacy and Data Protection

☐ Are GDPR data protection obligations reviewed periodically after deployment?

☐ Are controls in place to detect and prevent purpose creep?

Broader Review

☐ Does periodic review assess whether system benefits remain aligned with protections for affected people?

☐ Has a societal and environmental impact review been scheduled?

Shutdown and Decommissioning

☐ Are shutdown and decommissioning criteria defined and understood by accountable roles?

Why Oversight Defines Responsible AI

Governance, stakeholder inclusion, data responsibility, and transparency create the foundation.

Long-term oversight sustains it.

An AI system is not responsible because it was responsibly designed.

It is responsible because it remains accountable throughout its lifecycle.

Without oversight, initial safeguards erode.

With oversight, AI systems can adapt responsibly to changing conditions.

That is the difference between deployment and stewardship.

Part III

When AI Goes Wrong

Chapter 10

When Things Go Wrong

Artificial intelligence failures rarely begin with one technical mistake.

More often, harm grows through a chain of decisions made during design, development, deployment, and oversight. Weak governance, poor testing, weak data controls, limited transparency, and missing post-deployment monitoring can turn small problems into serious consequences.

When these controls fail, AI systems may work exactly as designed and still produce harmful, unfair, or legally risky outcomes.

The case studies in this section show how these failures occur in practice. Table 10.1 summarizes which pillars are implicated in each example.

Although these cases come from very different industries—retail, finance, law, and artificial intelligence development—they share a common pattern.

In each case, one or more of the Five Pillars of Moral AI Projects were weak or missing.

Table 10.1: Relationship between case studies and the Five Pillars of Moral AI Projects.

Case	Governance	Stakeholder Inclusion	Data Responsibility	Transparency & Explainability	Long-Term Oversight
Pharmacy-Facial Recognition	✓	✓	✓	✓	✓
Auto-Loan Algorithm	✓			✓	✓
Automated Trading	✓		✓	✓	✓
GenAI-Misuse	✓			✓	✓
Copyright-Use	✓	✓	✓	✓	✓

These pillars are not abstract ideas. They are practical safeguards that must be built into the AI project lifecycle.

The cases that follow show what happens when those safeguards are absent.

The cases presented in this chapter are derived from publicly available sources, including regulatory actions, court filings, and reported events. They are included solely to illustrate how the Five Pillars of Moral AI Projects can be applied to the examination of real-world AI project failures.

These summaries are not intended to provide legal analysis or definitive conclusions. The cases have been simplified for educational purposes, and some details may be incomplete, contested, or subject to differing interpretations.

Chapter 11

Pharmacy Facial Recognition Case

In 2023, the U.S. Federal Trade Commission (FTC) took action against a large American pharmacy chain for its use of facial recognition technology in retail stores (FTC, 2023).

The system was designed to identify people suspected of shoplifting. Instead, it became an example of how weak governance and poor testing can turn a security system into a source of harm.

This case shows how failures in data quality, testing, oversight, and governance can lead to serious consequences.

What Happened

The pharmacy deployed facial recognition software across hundreds of stores countrywide.

The system scanned customers' faces and compared them against a database of individuals flagged as potential security risks.

1. Weak ethical governance at the start
No clear ethics owner, no formal risk gate, and no documented accountability for harms.

2. Inadequate validation before deployment
Accuracy and error rates not rigorously tested, measured, or documented for real store conditions.

3. Poor input/data quality controls
Low-quality images and inconsistent capture conditions increase false matches.

4. Over-reliance on the system in operations
Alerts treated as "truth" instead of "signals"; unclear escalation and review steps.

5. Limited monitoring and feedback loops
False positives not consistently tracked, investigated, or used to improve the system.

6. Biased and unequal real-world impact
Higher false positives in certain communities; fairness checks missing or ineffective.

7. Harm to individuals and loss of trust
Public accusations, distress, police involvement, reputational damage.

8. Regulatory and business consequences
Enforcement action, bans/restrictions, mandated deletion, compliance costs, reputational fallout.

Figure 11.1: Failure Chain (The Pharmacy-Facial Recognition Case): How weak governance and controls can escalate into harm and enforcement action.

According to the FTC complaint, the system generated thousands of false matches.

In several cases:

- Customers were incorrectly identified as shoplifters

- Employees followed them through stores

- Customers were searched or asked to leave

- Police were called

- Individuals were accused in front of family members or other customers

Many of those flagged had never engaged in theft.

For those affected, the consequences were immediate and personal.

What Went Wrong

The failure was not caused by artificial intelligence alone. It resulted from weak governance and poor project controls across several areas.

Insufficient Testing Before Deployment

The organization did not properly test or document the accuracy of the system before deploying it.

Vendor claims about system performance were not independently verified.

Poor Data and Image Quality Controls

The system relied on low-quality images. Facial recognition is highly sensitive to image resolution, lighting, and camera angles.

Weak data quality increases the likelihood of false matches.

Weak Monitoring After Deployment

The company did not consistently track false positives once the system was operational.

Without monitoring, it was difficult to determine how often the system made mistakes.

Inadequate Human Oversight

Employees treated system alerts as confirmed evidence rather than as indicators requiring verification.

This led to customers being confronted or reported to the police based solely on algorithmic outputs.

Failure to Test for Bias

The FTC alleged that the system produced higher false positive rates in stores located in predominantly Black and Asian communities.

This suggests that the organization had not adequately evaluated differences in demographic performance before deployment.

Weak Data Governance

The FTC required the company to delete biometric data and implement stronger data protection policies.

This indicates weaknesses in data governance, consent processes, and retention policies.

Impact

The consequences were serious for both individuals and the organization.

Impact on Individuals

People who were incorrectly flagged experienced:

- Public embarrassment

- Emotional distress

- Reputational harm

- Police involvement without justification

For those involved, the incident was not a technical error. It was a personal crisis.

Impact on the Organization

The FTC banned the company from using facial recognition technology for five years.

The organization also faced:

- Regulatory enforcement

- Public scrutiny

- Reputational damage

- Operational disruption

Where the Project Failed

The project failed at several stages of the AI lifecycle.

1. The system was deployed without sufficient validation.
2. Vendor claims were not independently verified.
3. Data quality controls were weak.
4. Post-deployment monitoring was limited.
5. Employees were not trained to interpret AI outputs correctly.
6. Potential civil rights risks were not fully assessed.
7. Data governance and privacy controls were incomplete.

These failures formed a chain of preventable decisions.

Pillars Implicated

Several of the Five Pillars of Moral AI Projects were affected.

- **Governance.** Clear accountability for system testing, deployment decisions, and monitoring was missing.

- **Stakeholder Inclusion.** Customers affected by the system had no voice in how it was designed or deployed.

- **Data Responsibility.** Weak controls over image quality and biometric data governance increased the risk of false matches.

- **Transparency and Explainability.** Employees and customers had a limited understanding of how the system produced its alerts.

- **Long-Term Oversight.** The organization did not maintain effective monitoring of system performance after deployment.

Lessons for AI Project Teams

Several lessons emerge from this case.

- AI systems should not be deployed without documented validation of accuracy.

- Vendor claims should be independently verified.

- False positives must be continuously monitored and audited.

- Employees must understand the limits of AI systems.

- Systems that affect civil rights require bias testing.

- Biometric data requires strong governance and privacy protection.

A Leadership Failure

This case was not simply a technical failure.

It reflected weaknesses in governance, oversight, and risk awareness.

Technology amplified the consequences, but leadership decisions created the conditions for failure.

Deploying AI systems is not only a technical milestone. It is also a leadership decision with ethical implications.

When systems affect reputation, liberty, or civil rights, governance must be treated as a core responsibility rather than an afterthought.

Chapter 12

The Auto Loan Algorithm Case

Financial institutions increasingly rely on algorithms to calculate credit exposure and portfolio performance.

These systems can improve speed and consistency. However, when governance and oversight are weak, algorithmic errors can spread rapidly across many transactions.

This case shows how the absence of lifecycle governance and monitoring allowed known defects to persist within an operational financial system ("Walter Auto Loan Tr. v. Track Motors, LLC", 2023).

What Happened

A financial technology organization deployed a proprietary algorithm to calculate borrowing bases for automobile dealerships participating in a financing program.

Dealerships sold portfolios of vehicle loans to the organization in exchange for financing. The algorithm determined how much capital could be advanced and how repayments and buybacks affected borrowing capacity.

1. Weak governance at deployment
No clear accountability for transparent calculation logic or defect response.

↓

2. Opaque calculation process
Dealerships could not verify how borrowing-base results were produced.

↓

3. Known defects not corrected
The algorithm continued in use despite alleged calculation errors.

↓

4. Weak post-deployment monitoring
Anomalies in financial calculations were not systematically detected or escalated.

↓

5. No effective remediation loop
Operational feedback did not trigger redesign, correction, or stronger controls.

↓

6. Financial harm to dealerships
Funds were allegedly withheld, affecting cash flow and borrowing capacity.

↓

7. Legal and reputational consequences
Litigation, scrutiny, and questions about governance followed.

↓

8. Governance lesson
Financial algorithms require transparency, monitoring, and continuous oversight.

Figure 12.1: Failure Chain (Auto-Loan Algorithm Case): Weak governance, limited transparency, and poor post-deployment oversight allowed calculation defects to persist and escalate into financial harm and litigation.

Dealerships later alleged that the algorithm contained calculation errors that caused funds owed to them to be improperly withheld.

In one example cited in the litigation, more than $100,000 was allegedly withheld from a single loan portfolio due to calculation errors.

According to the allegations, the organization was aware of these defects but continued to use the system without correction.

Dealerships also claimed that the system lacked transparency and that they could not independently verify how the algorithm calculated financial outcomes.

What Went Wrong

The failure resulted from weaknesses in governance and system oversight.

Several issues contributed to the problem.

Lack of Calculation Transparency.

The algorithm's financial calculations could not be easily verified by participating dealerships. Without transparent logic or traceable outputs, stakeholders could not validate the system's results.

Failure to Correct Known Defects.

Once defects were identified, the organization did not immediately redesign or correct the algorithm. The system continued to operate despite known errors.

Weak Post-Deployment Monitoring.

The organization did not implement adequate monitoring mechanisms to detect anomalies in financial calculations.

Without monitoring, errors remained embedded in operational processes.

Absence of Feedback and Remediation Processes.

Operational problems did not trigger a structured remediation process. There was no clear pathway for correcting the system once defects became visible.

Impact

The consequences affected both the dealerships and the organization.

Impact on Dealerships

Dealerships alleged that funds owed to them were improperly withheld.

These errors affected their:

- Cash flow

- Borrowing capacity

- Financial stability

Because the algorithm's calculations were not transparent, dealerships could not verify the accuracy of financial outcomes.

Impact on the Organization

The dispute resulted in litigation alleging unfair or deceptive practices.

The organization also faced:

- Legal scrutiny

- Reputational risk

- Questions about governance of its financial technology systems

Where the Project Failed

The project failed across several stages of the system lifecycle.

1. The algorithm was deployed without transparent or auditable calculation logic.
2. Known system defects did not trigger redesign or corrective action.
3. Post-deployment monitoring mechanisms were weak or absent.
4. Operational feedback did not lead to system improvements.

The problem was not only that the algorithm contained errors. It was that governance structures were too weak to respond once those errors were discovered.

Pillars Implicated

- **Governance.** Clear accountability for algorithm design, validation, and defect remediation was not established.

- **Stakeholder Inclusion.** Dealerships had limited ability to review or challenge algorithmic calculations.

- **Data Responsibility.** Financial calculations relied on algorithmic processes that lacked adequate validation and control.

- **Transparency and Explainability.** Stakeholders could not independently verify how the system produced borrowing base calculations.

- **Long-Term Oversight.** The organization did not implement adequate monitoring or feedback mechanisms after deployment.

Lessons for AI Project Teams

Several lessons emerge from this case.

- Algorithms used in financial decision-making must provide traceable calculation logic.

- Known defects must trigger immediate remediation and system redesign.

- Post-deployment monitoring is essential for detecting anomalies in operational systems.

- Stakeholders affected by algorithmic decisions should be able to review and verify outcomes.

- Governance processes must continue to remain active throughout the system lifecycle, not end at launch.

Algorithmic systems can scale financial errors rapidly when lifecycle governance is weak.

A Leadership Failure

This case reflects more than a technical defect.

It reveals weaknesses in leadership oversight and governance discipline.

Leaders responsible for deploying algorithmic systems must ensure that monitoring, defect management, and continuous improvement remain active after deployment.

Without these safeguards, small design flaws can grow into systemic financial disputes.

Technology did not create the failure. Weak governance allowed it to persist.

Chapter 13
Automated Trading Case

Automated trading systems operate in financial environments where decisions occur in milliseconds and financial exposure can escalate rapidly.

Because of this speed and scale, these systems must be designed, tested, and validated with exceptional rigor before they are deployed in live markets.

This case illustrates how weaknesses in algorithm design, data preparation, and validation can produce substantial financial harm when project quality controls are insufficient ("Batchelar v. Interactive Brokers, LLC", 2019).

What Happened

An investor held a margin account with an online brokerage platform that used an automated liquidation algorithm to manage risk.

Margin accounts require investors to maintain a minimum level of collateral; when an account falls below required thresholds, the brokerage platform may automatically sell securities to restore compliance.

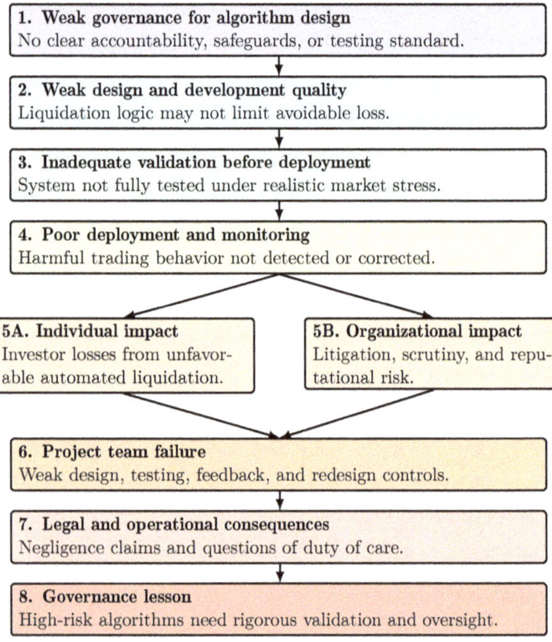

Figure 13.1: Failure Chain (Automated Trading Case): weak design, validation, deployment, and monitoring can lead to both investor harm and organizational consequences before converging in a broader project team failure.

The investor alleged that the platform's liquidation algorithm triggered a sequence of automated trades that rapidly sold positions in his account.

According to the allegations, the liquidation sequence resulted in losses significantly greater than those that would normally occur under controlled trading conditions.

The investor argued that the algorithm had not been properly designed, developed, or tested, and that flaws in the system caused trades to be executed at prices far below prevailing market values.

The case raised questions about whether those responsible for the design and operation of the algorithm had exercised reasonable care in developing and deploying the system.

What Went Wrong

Several weaknesses in project quality controls contributed to the failure.

Design Weaknesses.

The liquidation algorithm may not have included safeguards to limit avoidable financial harm during forced liquidations.

Effective trading algorithms often use staged liquidation strategies, price monitoring, and execution controls to reduce losses.

Development and Implementation Gaps.

Automated trading systems require safeguards that prevent cascading trades or excessive market impact.

The allegations suggest that these protections may have been insufficient.

Data Preparation Limitations.

Trading algorithms depend on accurate and representative market data.

If development datasets do not reflect real market volatility, liquidity conditions, and trading constraints, algorithm behavior in live markets may diverge significantly from expected outcomes.

Validation and Testing Failures.

High-risk financial systems require extensive validation before deployment.

Simulation environments, stress testing, and volatility scenarios should be used to evaluate algorithm behavior under extreme conditions.

The allegations suggest that the system may not have undergone sufficient validation before being deployed in live trading.

Impact

The consequences affected both the investor and the organization operating the platform.

Impact on the Investor

The investor alleged that the liquidation process caused his positions to be sold at prices significantly below market prices.

As a result, the investor experienced losses that may have been avoidable if the algorithm had executed trades more carefully.

Impact on the Organization

The dispute led to litigation examining whether the brokerage platform and its developers had exercised reasonable care in designing and operating the system.

The case also raised broader concerns about governance practices for automated financial systems.

For organizations operating algorithmic trading platforms, such disputes can create both regulatory attention and reputational risk.

Where the Project Failed

The project failed at multiple stages of the system lifecycle.

1. The liquidation logic may not have been designed to limit financial harm during forced trades.
2. Development data and market scenarios may not have accurately reflected real-world trading environments.
3. Validation and stress testing may have been insufficient prior to deployment.
4. Monitoring mechanisms may not have been strong enough to detect harmful trading behavior after deployment.

These weaknesses allowed the algorithm to operate in a high-risk financial environment without sufficient safeguards.

Pillars Implicated

- **Governance.** Accountability for algorithm design, validation, and operational safeguards was not clearly established.

- **Stakeholder Inclusion.** Investors affected by automated trading decisions had little insight into how liquidation rules operated.

- **Data Responsibility.** Development datasets and market simulations may not have adequately represented real trading conditions.

- **Transparency and Explainability.** Investors had limited ability to understand how the algorithm determined liquidation timing and execution.

- **Long-Term Oversight.** Monitoring and performance review mechanisms were insufficient to identify harmful behavior once the system was active.

Lessons for AI Project Teams

The Automated Trading Case highlights several lessons for teams building high-risk algorithmic systems.

- Algorithms operating in financial markets require rigorous validation before deployment.

- Design safeguards should minimize unnecessary financial harm during automated actions.

- Development datasets and simulations must reflect real operating environments.

- Monitoring systems must detect abnormal behavior after deployment.

- Governance processes must ensure that automated systems remain accountable to human oversight.

Automated systems increase both the speed and scale of decision-making. Without careful controls, they also increase the scale of potential errors.

A Leadership Failure

This case illustrates the responsibilities that accompany automation in high-risk environments.

Leaders who authorize automated financial systems must ensure that robust quality controls are in place across design, testing, and operational monitoring.

When systems operate at machine speed, governance and validation must operate with equal discipline.

Failure to build those controls into the project lifecycle can expose both investors and organizations to significant financial risk.

Chapter 14

Generative AI Misuse Case

AI failures do not occur only when automated systems make decisions about people.

They can also occur when AI tools are introduced into professional workflows without clear governance, safeguards, or user awareness.

In this case, attorneys submitted a legal brief containing judicial opinions that did not exist. The citations had been generated by a generative AI (GenAI) system used to assist with legal research ("Mata v. Avianca, Inc." 2023).

The incident illustrates how risks can emerge when generative AI (GenAI) tools are used in professional environments without appropriate verification processes.

What Happened

Attorneys representing a plaintiff in litigation against an airline submitted a legal brief opposing a motion to dismiss.

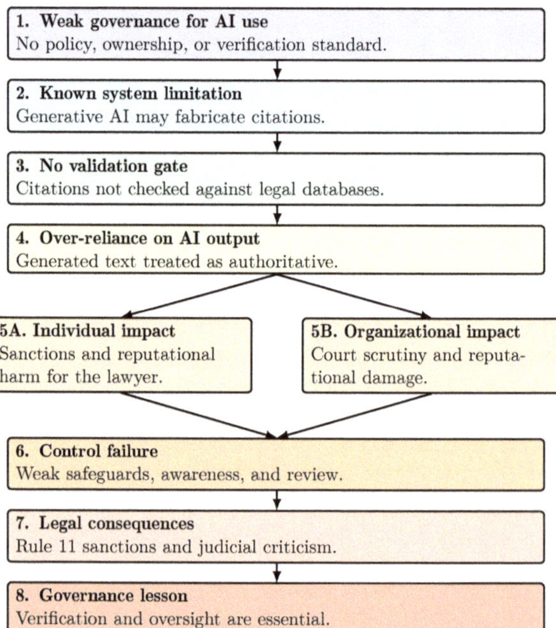

Figure 14.1: Failure Chain (GenAI–Misuse Case): AI-assisted work without governance, verification, and oversight can lead to both individual and organizational consequences.

The brief cited several judicial opinions intended to support the plaintiff's argument. When opposing counsel attempted to locate the cited cases, they discovered that several decisions could not be found in any legal database.

The citations had been generated by an AI system the attorneys used for legal research.

When the court asked for copies of the cited opinions, the lawyers submitted additional documents containing quotations and citations that were also fabricated.

The court ultimately determined that the referenced cases did not exist.

The attorneys later acknowledged that they had relied on the AI system to generate research results and had not independently verified the citations before filing.

What Went Wrong

Several failures contributed to the incident.

Unverified AI Outputs.

The attorneys relied on AI-generated citations without confirming their existence in authoritative legal databases.

Professional research standards require independent verification before legal sources are submitted to a court.

Known Limitations of GenAI

GenAI systems can produce fabricated information, commonly referred to as "hallucinations." These systems generate text based on language patterns rather than verified facts.

Without verification safeguards, plausible but incorrect outputs can appear convincing.

Lack of Governance Policies.

No formal policies governed how AI tools could be used in legal research or document preparation.

Without such guidance, attorneys relied on AI outputs beyond the system's reliable capabilities.

Absence of Review Procedures.

No internal review process existed to validate AI-assisted research before the filing was submitted to the court.

A basic verification step would likely have prevented the incident.

Impact

Although the case did not involve automated decisions about individuals, the consequences were significant.

Impact on the Legal Process

The submission of fabricated judicial opinions disrupted court proceedings and required the judge to investigate the authenticity of the citations.

Court resources were spent resolving an issue that should have been prevented through basic verification.

Impact on the Attorneys

The court sanctioned the attorneys under Rule 11 of the Federal Rules of Civil Procedure and imposed a financial penalty.

The case received widespread attention from professionals and the media, raising concerns about the responsible use of GenAI in legal practice.

For professionals whose credibility is essential to their work, reputational consequences can be severe.

Where the Project Failed

Several governance gaps allowed the incident to occur.

1. No organizational policies defined the appropriate use of AI tools in legal research.
2. The AI system produced authoritative-looking citations without integrated verification mechanisms.
3. Users were not trained to recognize known failure modes of generative AI.
4. No review or validation process was followed before AI-generated information was submitted in court filings.

These failures demonstrate how risks can emerge when AI tools are introduced into professional work environments without appropriate controls.

Pillars Implicated

- **Governance.** No formal policies or accountability structures were in place to guide the use of AI tools in legal research.

- **Stakeholder Inclusion.** Courts and opposing counsel were indirectly affected by AI-generated content that had not been verified.

- **Data Responsibility.** AI-generated information was treated as reliable without verifying its accuracy against authoritative sources.

- **Transparency and Explainability.** Users did not fully understand the system's limitations regarding factual accuracy.

- **Long-Term Oversight.** No review process existed to validate AI-generated outputs before their use in court filings.

Lessons for AI Project Teams

This case highlights several lessons for organizations introducing GenAI tools into professional environments.

- AI-generated outputs must be verified before being treated as authoritative information.

- Systems should clearly communicate known limitations, especially regarding factual accuracy.

- Interfaces should encourage verification rather than passive acceptance of generated results.

- Organizations should establish governance policies defining acceptable uses of AI tools.

- Professional workflows should include review processes when AI-generated content is used.

GenAI can accelerate research and drafting, but it does not replace professional judgment or verification.

A Leadership Failure

This case illustrates a broader challenge associated with introducing AI tools into professional environments.

Leaders who adopt new technologies must also ensure that the associated processes, training, and governance structures evolve at the same pace.

Without clear guidance, users may assume that AI systems provide reliable outputs even when those systems are designed only to generate plausible text.

Responsible adoption of AI, therefore, requires not only technical capability but also clear policies, education, and oversight to guide professionals in using the technology safely.

Chapter 15
Copyright Use Case

AI systems depend heavily on the data used to train them.

When datasets are collected without clear controls over provenance, ownership, and permitted use, legal and ethical risks can become embedded in the system from the outset.

This case illustrates how weaknesses in dataset preparation and governance can expose organizations to large-scale legal and reputational risk ("Bartz v. Anthropic PBC", 2025).

What Happened

The authors alleged that an AI developer downloaded millions of copyrighted books from unauthorized online repositories and used them to construct training datasets for large language models.

Engineers reportedly automated the collection of digital books from large online libraries known to contain unauthorized copies of copyrighted works.

These downloads occurred at scale, producing a dataset of millions of books.

Project Failure Points

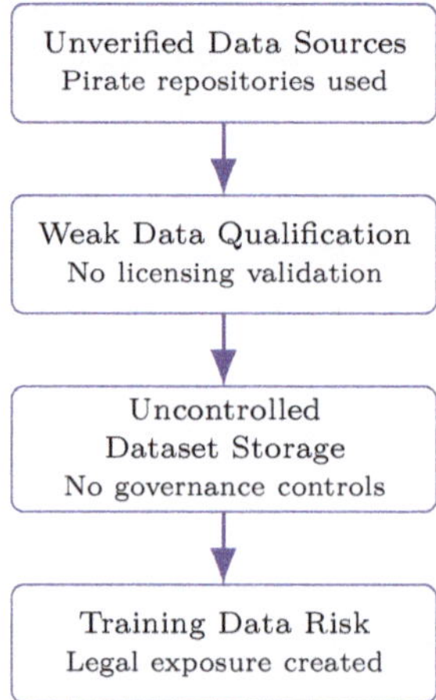

Figure 15.1: Key project governance breakdown points in the Copyright–Use case.

The files were then stored in internal repositories for experimentation, analysis, and model training.

Although the legal dispute focused on copyright law, the broader issue concerned how training datasets were collected and governed.

The case raised questions about whether the organization had implemented sufficient controls to verify the origin and legal status of the data used to train its models.

What Went Wrong

Several weaknesses in data governance contributed to the problem.

Unqualified Data Sources.

The dataset included material obtained from repositories known to contain unauthorized copies of copyrighted works.

There was no evidence that these sources were formally validated before use in AI development.

Weak Dataset Governance.

Large collections of downloaded books were stored internally without clear governance mechanisms defining ownership rights, licensing status, or permitted use.

Without structured dataset governance, ensuring legally compliant data use becomes difficult.

Limited Data Provenance Controls.

Metadata associated with the files could identify titles and sources, but appears to have been used primarily for technical management rather than for verifying copyright status or usage rights.

Effective dataset governance requires provenance controls that support both engineering and compliance needs.

Failure to Assess Data Preparation Risk.

Training datasets are a foundational component of AI systems.

If the dataset contains improperly sourced material, the resulting model inherits the legal and ethical risks associated with that data.

The absence of structured dataset qualification processes allowed these risks to remain embedded throughout development.

Impact

The consequences were significant for both the organization and the broader AI ecosystem.

Impact on Rights Holders.

Authors and publishers alleged that their copyrighted works were used without permission in the training dataset.

This raised concerns about intellectual property rights and the treatment of creative works in AI development.

Impact on the Organization.

The organization faced large-scale litigation involving many authors and publishers.

Because copyright damages may be assessed per infringed work, the case exposed the organization to substantial financial risk.

The dispute also created reputational challenges and increased public scrutiny of how AI companies acquire training data.

Finally, the litigation introduced operational uncertainty. If an AI system is trained on improperly sourced data, organizations may ultimately need to rebuild datasets, retrain models, or redesign systems to reduce legal exposure.

Where the Project Failed

The failure occurred during the early stages of the AI lifecycle, particularly during dataset preparation.

1. Data sources were collected without formal validation of licensing or ownership.
2. Dataset governance mechanisms defining permitted use were incomplete.
3. Data provenance controls did not adequately support legal verification.
4. Project risk assessments did not fully evaluate intellectual property exposure.

These weaknesses allowed legal risk to become embedded in the training dataset before the model was even developed.

Pillars Implicated

- **Governance.** Oversight mechanisms for dataset sourcing and licensing verification were insufficient.

- **Stakeholder Inclusion.** Authors and publishers whose works formed part of the dataset were not included in decisions about how their content would be used.

- **Data Responsibility.** Training data was collected without adequate controls over provenance, licensing status, and permitted use.

- **Transparency and Explainability.** There was limited transparency about the origin and composition of the datasets used to train the system.

- **Long-Term Oversight.** Ongoing review of dataset legality and compliance risks appears to have been limited after the data was collected.

Lessons for AI Project Teams

The Copyright-Use Case highlights several lessons for organizations developing AI systems.

- Data preparation is one of the highest-risk stages of AI development.

- Training datasets must include documented provenance and licensing information.

- Automated data collection can scale legal exposure as quickly as it scales technical capability.

- Metadata should support governance and compliance verification, not only engineering tasks.

- Intellectual property risks must be evaluated during dataset construction.

Responsible AI development begins with responsible data acquisition.

A Leadership Failure

This case highlights the governance challenges that arise when innovation outpaces oversight.

Leaders responsible for AI development must ensure that dataset acquisition follows the same standards of accountability applied to other critical business assets.

Training data is not simply a technical resource. It is a foundational component of the system that carries legal, ethical, and reputational implications.

Organizations that fail to govern their data sources risk embedding those liabilities directly into the technologies they create.

Part IV

Implementation and Leadership

Chapter 16

Implementation Roadmap: Embedding the Five Pillars into AI Projects

16.1 From Framework to Execution

The Five Pillars define what responsible AI requires.

The implementation roadmap defines how to embed those pillars into real project structures.

AI projects do not operate in isolation. They are executed within organizational governance systems that include:

- Project sponsors

- Project managers

- Project teams

- Risk and compliance functions

- Executive oversight bodies

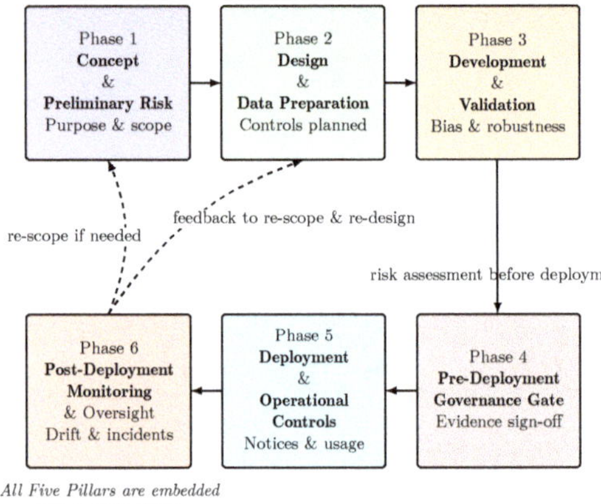

Figure 16.1: Implementation Roadmap. The six phases of responsible AI project delivery: Phase 1, Concept and Risk Classification; Phase 2, Design and Data Preparation; Phase 3, Development and Validation; Phase 4, Pre-Deployment Governance Gate; Phase 5, Deployment and Operational Controls; and Phase 6, Post-Market Monitoring and Continuous Oversight.

To be effective, moral AI governance must align with these existing structures rather than operate parallel to them.

16.2 The AI Project Implementation Roadmap

Phase 1: Concept and Risk Classification

Before development begins, teams must:

- Define the intended system purpose

- Identify affected stakeholders

- Conduct a preliminary risk assessment

- Determine EU AI Act risk category

- Assess GDPR implications

At this stage:

- Governance structure must be defined

- A stakeholder inclusion plan must be drafted

- Budget must be allocated for governance controls.

High-risk classification under the EU AI Act triggers enhanced obligations.

Failure to classify correctly at this stage may result in non-compliance later.

Phase 2: Design and Data Preparation

During design, teams must:

- Define decision rights and approval gates

- Conduct stakeholder mapping

- Establish data sourcing controls

- Verify lawful basis and licensing

- Plan transparency mechanisms

ISO-aligned quality management processes should incorporate:

- Documentation checkpoints

- Bias testing protocols

- Data protection impact assessments where required

This phase embeds Pillars 1–3 most heavily.

Phase 3: Development and Validation

During model development, teams must:

- Execute bias and robustness testing

- Validate across demographic and intersectional groups

- Document model logic and limitations

- Conduct internal technical review

For high-risk systems, technical documentation must satisfy EU AI Act requirements for traceability and auditability.

Validation must not be limited to technical accuracy. It must include fairness, explainability, and regulatory alignment.

Risk Assessment Before Deployment

Under the EU AI Act, high-risk AI systems require formal risk management and conformity assessment before being placed on the market or put into service.

Even where regulation does not mandate it, conducting a structured pre-deployment risk assessment represents sound governance practice.

This assessment functions as the transition point from pre-production to operational deployment and marks a critical governance milestone in the project lifecycle.

Importantly, risk assessment should not rely on autonomy labels alone. Governance intensity should instead be calibrated to actual system capabilities, decision reach, opacity, and operational risk.

Before deployment, organizations must:

- Conduct a documented risk assessment covering health, safety, and fundamental rights

- Identify foreseeable misuse and unintended consequences

- Implement risk mitigation measures

- Verify technical documentation completeness

- Confirm human oversight mechanisms

- Validate data governance controls

- Ensure transparency obligations are satisfied

Risk assessment is not a technical formality.

It is a governance checkpoint.

Deployment without a documented risk assessment exposes the organization to regulatory penalties and reputational harm.

The pre-deployment phase must therefore include a formal sign-off confirming that:

- Risk classification has been verified

- Mitigation measures are implemented

- Residual risks are acceptable

- Accountability is clearly assigned

Risk assessment forms the bridge between system development and lawful deployment.

Phase 4: Pre-Deployment Governance Gate

Before deployment, organizations must:

- Confirm documentation completeness

- Validate stakeholder protections

- Confirm human oversight mechanisms,

- Verify transparency disclosures

- Obtain formal sponsor approval

This governance gate formalizes accountability.

Deployment without formal sign-off weakens compliance defensibility.

Phase 5: Deployment and Operational Controls

At deployment, teams must:

- Activate monitoring mechanisms

- Enable incident reporting channels

- Communicate user-level transparency notices

- Implement usage controls

Under the EU AI Act, providers must ensure that systems are used according to instructions and that monitoring continues after release.

Operational controls extend beyond launch.

Phase 6: Post-Market Monitoring and Continuous Oversight

After deployment, teams must:

- Track performance and bias metrics

- Conduct periodic compliance reviews

- Monitor societal impact indicators

- Govern retraining cycles formally

- Report serious incidents where required

Oversight must be scheduled, documented, and reviewed at the executive level.

Governance evolves with system use, operational experience, and regulatory expectations.

In practice, post-deployment monitoring most often triggers iteration in design, data preparation, validation, and operational controls (Phases 2–6).

A return to Phase 1 is required only when the system's purpose, risk boundaries, or stakeholder impacts materially change.

16.3 Governance Integration

Aligning with Project Roles

Clear role alignment prevents accountability diffusion.

The following high-level role structure reflects common ISO-aligned project environments:

Project Sponsor

- Owns strategic intent

- Carries ultimate accountability

- Approves risk thresholds and deployment decisions

- Ensures resource allocation for governance controls

Project Manager

- Integrates governance requirements into delivery plans

- Coordinates stakeholder inclusion activities

- Ensures documentation and checkpoints are completed

- Escalates risks to sponsors or governance bodies

Project Team

- Implements data controls

- Conducts bias testing

- Documents model characteristics

- Supports explainability mechanisms

Risk, Legal, and Compliance Functions

- Reviews regulatory obligations

- Validates documentation completeness

- Confirms lawful basis for data processing

- Advises on high-risk classification

Independent Oversight or Ethics Committee (where applicable)

- Reviews high-risk design choices

- Assesses societal and stakeholder impact

- Advises on deployment readiness

Each pillar must be explicitly assigned across these roles.

If ownership is unclear, governance weakens.

Master Responsibility Matrix

```
Pillar                Sp  PM  Tech  Comp  Ovs
--------------------------------------------------
Governance            A   R   C     C     I
Stakeholder Incl.     A   R   C     C     C
Data Responsibility   I   C   R     A     C
Transparency          I   R   C     A     C
Long-Term Oversight   A   R   C     C     R

Sp=Sponsor PM=ProjectMgr Tech=Technical
Comp=Compliance Ovs=Oversight
R=Responsible A=Accountable C=Consulted I=Informed
```

This matrix prevents accountability diffusion.

Each pillar must have a named accountable role. Shared responsibility without ownership weakens governance.

Integration with ISO Standards

Organizations operating under ISO/IEC 42001-aligned management systems can embed the Five Pillars within:

- Risk management processes

- Quality assurance checkpoints

- Internal audit cycles

- Change management procedures

- Management review meetings

The Five Pillars do not replace existing governance frameworks.

They enhance them for AI-specific risk.

16.4 Oversight and Organizational Accountability

Board-Level Oversight

For high-risk or large-scale AI systems, board-level visibility is advisable.

Executive reporting should include:

- Risk classification

- Stakeholder impact summary

- Bias and fairness metrics

- Incident reporting status

- Regulatory compliance posture

Board oversight reinforces accountability at the highest level.

16.5   Using the Implementation Tools

Implementing the Five Pillars requires more than conceptual alignment. Organizations must be able to assess whether governance structures are actually functioning in practice.

Two practical tools are provided in the appendices to support this process.

Appendix A, the AI Governance Readiness Scoring Model, provides a maturity rubric covering two sections. Section 1 evaluates the strength of controls across the Five Pillars. Section 2 evaluates the maturity of implementation practices and leadership culture described in this chapter and Chapter 17. Each section is scored independently so that strengths in one area do not mask weaknesses in another. The combined scores can be plotted on the governance matrix in Appendix A to identify the organization's current governance profile and priority areas for improvement.

Appendix B, the AI Ethical Readiness Scorecard, provides a structured worksheet for use during governance reviews, project gates, or internal audits.

The roadmap explains *how responsible AI should be implemented*. The appendices help determine *whether it actually has been*.

Implementation Readiness Checklist

Governance Structure

☐ Are roles assigned for each of the Five Pillars?

☐ Are governance gates embedded in the project?

☐ Is executive oversight structured, recurring, and documented?

Documentation and Regulatory Alignment

☐ Is documentation audit-ready across all pillar areas?

☐ Is EU AI Act risk classification recorded and verified by the compliance function?

Monitoring and Maturity

☐ Are post-market monitoring processes defined before deployment?

☐ Does governance exist at the organizational level, not only at the project level?

☐ Has the AI Governance Readiness Scoring Model in Appendix A been completed and reviewed?

☐ Has the governance matrix been used to identify the current profile and priority improvement areas?

Why the Roadmap Matters

Ethical AI cannot rely on individual heroics.

It requires an institutional structure.

The implementation roadmap ensures that:

- Responsibility is assigned,

- Risk is documented

- Compliance is verifiable

- Oversight is continuous

The Five Pillars define what responsible AI requires.

The roadmap ensures it is delivered.

Chapter 17

Leadership and Culture

17.1 Structure Is Necessary. Culture Is Decisive.

The Five Pillars provide structure.

The implementation roadmap embeds that structure into project processes.

But structure alone does not ensure responsible AI.

Organizational culture determines whether governance mechanisms are respected, bypassed, or quietly weakened.

Leadership determines whether ethics is operational or rhetorical.

The cases described in Chapters 10–15 illustrate how weaknesses in leadership culture can undermine governance structures. Table 17.1 highlights how the leadership practices described in this chapter could have mitigated the failures observed in those cases.

Table 17.1: Leadership Culture and AI Project Failures: Case-Based Comparison

Leadership Factor	Case Example	Observed Failure	Leadership Mitigation
Tone at the Top	Pharmacy Facial Recognition	Deployment prioritized loss prevention over accuracy and civil rights risk.	Executives require validation evidence and fairness testing before deployment approval.
Incentives and Ethical Drift	Pharmacy Facial Recognition	Store performance incentives encouraged aggressive use of system alerts.	Align incentives so teams are rewarded for responsible use and escalation of system errors.
Moral Disengagement	Lawyer Misuse Case	Attorneys relied on AI-generated citations without verifying authenticity.	Leaders reinforce that AI outputs require professional verification and judgment.
Social Drift	Pharmacy Facial Recognition	Governance safeguards weakened as the system scaled across stores.	Maintain required validation and monitoring processes even under operational pressure.
Diffusion of Accountability	Auto-Loan Algorithm Case	Responsibility for algorithm defects and remediation was unclear across teams.	Assign explicit accountability for algorithm validation, monitoring, and redesign.

Continued on next page

Table 17.1 – continued from previous page

Leadership Factor	Case Example	Observed Failure	Leadership Mitigation
Human Oversight Culture	Pharmacy Facial Recognition	Employees treated system alerts as definitive rather than signals.	Train personnel to interpret AI outputs critically and empower overrides.
Transparency Discipline	Auto-Loan Algorithm Case	Dealerships could not understand how financial calculations were generated.	Require explainable calculation logic and transparent reporting of outcomes.
Data Responsibility Leadership	Copyright-Use Case	Large-scale datasets were assembled without verifying copyright legitimacy.	Require formal data provenance checks and legal review before dataset ingestion.
Validation and Testing Discipline	Automated Trading Case	Algorithm allegedly deployed without sufficient design validation or stress testing.	Required documented proof of rigorous simulation and validation before deploying high-risk algorithms.
Board-Level Oversight	Multiple Cases	Strategic oversight of AI risk and system monitoring was limited.	Boards review risk classifications, fairness metrics, and post-deployment monitoring reports.
Ethical Courage	Multiple Cases	Systems continued operating despite visible risks or defects.	Leadership must be willing to delay deployment or redesign systems when risks appear.

17.2   Leadership and Ethical Behavior

The Limits of Formal Accountability

Formal accountability charts do not guarantee ethical behavior.

Research shows that in AI projects, accountability often becomes diffuse. Roles overlap. Responsibilities blur. Difficult decisions are delayed.

When leadership does not reinforce governance expectations, teams prioritize delivery over governance.

Deadlines override review. Performance metrics override caution. Efficiency overrides reflection.

An ethical leadership culture bridges the gap between written policy and actual behavior.

Tone at the Top

Leadership signals priorities through:

- What is measured

- What is rewarded

- What is questioned

- What is ignored

If executives ask only about speed and financial return, governance will weaken.

If executives regularly ask:

- What risks remain?

- Which stakeholders are affected?

- How confident is the team in fairness testing?

- What would justify pausing deployment?

ethical discipline strengthens.

Ethical AI requires visible leadership engagement, not silent endorsement.

Incentives and Ethical Drift

AI teams operate within performance systems.

If rewards depend primarily on delivery timelines or cost reduction, ethical review becomes secondary.

This creates ethical drift.

Ethical drift does not begin with misconduct. It begins with small compromises:

- "We will test that later."

- "The risk seems low."

- "We need to move quickly."

Over time, those compromises accumulate.

Leadership must align incentives with governance expectations.

Responsible behavior must be recognized, not penalized.

Leading Responsibility Under Delivery Pressure

AI projects rarely operate under ideal conditions.

Teams face deadlines, budget constraints, and pressure to demonstrate progress.

These pressures are normal in project environments, but they can weaken ethical discipline if leaders do not actively manage them.

Under strong delivery pressure, three patterns often emerge: moral disengagement, social drift, and diffusion of accountability.

These dynamics rarely begin with deliberate misconduct.

They develop gradually when responsibility becomes secondary to speed.

Moral Disengagement

Moral disengagement occurs when individuals separate technical work from its real-world consequences.

Developers may focus only on whether a system functions. Data teams may concentrate on processing data rather than questioning its origin. Product teams may prioritize performance metrics while overlooking fairness or societal impact.

Under delivery pressure, these narrow perspectives can intensify.

When success is measured only by speed or performance, ethical considerations appear secondary.

Leadership must actively counter this separation between technical work and responsibility.

Leaders reinforce engagement by asking:

- Who could be harmed by this system?

- What assumptions are being made about the data?

- What risks remain unresolved?

When leaders consistently connect technical decisions to real-world consequences, moral disengagement becomes far less likely.

Social Drift

Social drift occurs when small compromises gradually become accepted practice.

A validation step may be skipped once to meet a deadline. A dataset may be used without full documentation. A fairness test may be postponed.

Each decision seems minor.

But repeated compromises slowly redefine what teams consider acceptable.

Delivery pressure accelerates this process.

Governance steps begin to look like obstacles rather than safeguards.

Leadership must prevent shortcuts from becoming norms.

Consistent governance checkpoints, independent reviews, and clear documentation standards help maintain discipline.

Responsible practice must remain the default, even when deadlines approach.

Diffusion of Accountability

AI systems are rarely built by a single individual.

Developers write models. Engineers manage infrastructure. Data teams prepare datasets. Product managers define requirements. Executives approve deployment.

When many actors are involved, responsibility can become unclear.

Individuals may assume someone else is responsible for verifying data sources, validating models, or evaluating ethical risks.

This is diffusion of accountability.

Leadership must prevent it by clearly assigning responsibility for critical decisions.

Effective governance requires:

- Defined ownership for data governance

- Named responsibility for model validation

- Clear authority for deployment approval

- Documented decision records

When responsibility is visible, accountability becomes real.

Balancing Speed and Responsibility

Responsible leadership does not mean slowing innovation.

It means ensuring that delivery pressures do not silently weaken governance.

Leaders must reinforce that responsible practices are part of project success.

Not optional steps.

Not bureaucratic overhead.

But essential safeguards.

When responsible behavior is recognized and supported, teams maintain ethical discipline even under pressure.

Psychological Safety and Escalation

Governance frameworks assume that risks will be escalated.

But escalation requires psychological safety.

Team members must feel able to:

- Raise bias concerns

- Question model performance

- Challenge deployment readiness

- Report potential misuse

If raising concerns is perceived as a career risk, oversight mechanisms have failed.

Ethical culture requires that speaking up is both protected and expected.

17.3 Oversight and Organizational Responsibility

Human Oversight as a Cultural Practice

Regulatory frameworks such as the EU AI Act require human oversight.

But human oversight is not merely procedural.

It is cultural.

Effective oversight requires:

- Individuals trained to interpret AI outputs

- Authority to override system recommendations

- Clear documentation of intervention decisions

- Leadership support when overrides occur

If humans are formally "in the loop" but practically discouraged from intervening, oversight is symbolic.

Transparency as Leadership Discipline

Transparency as Leadership Discipline

Transparency requires leaders to accept scrutiny.

Documented limitations. Recorded bias metrics. Clear performance boundaries.

Leaders must model comfort with disclosure.

Defensive leadership culture suppresses transparency.

Mature leadership culture strengthens it.

Board-Level Responsibility

For high-risk AI systems, responsibility extends to the board.

Boards should request regular reporting on:

- Risk classification

- Bias and fairness metrics

- Incident reporting trends

- Regulatory developments

- Post-market monitoring results

AI governance is not a technical issue.

It is a strategic issue.

Board engagement reinforces that seriousness.

17.4   Building an Ethical Culture

Ethical Courage

Responsible AI sometimes requires difficult decisions:

- Delaying deployment

- Redesigning models

- Rejecting profitable use cases

- Decommissioning systems

These decisions may conflict with short-term performance goals.

Ethical courage distinguishes governance from compliance.

Compliance avoids penalties. Governance protects long-term legitimacy.

Cultural Signals of Maturity

Organizations demonstrating strong ethical culture typically:

- Hold regular governance review meetings

- Maintain transparent reporting structures

- Encourage cross-functional collaboration

- Involve independent oversight

- Demonstrate a continuous improvement mindset

They treat AI governance as institutional infrastructure, not a project overhead.

17.5   Leadership Tools for Responsible AI

Leaders play a critical role in ensuring that governance mechanisms are not treated as symbolic controls. The AI Governance Readiness Scoring Model in Appendix A and the AI Ethical Readiness Scorecard in Appendix B provide practical tools for leadership oversight.

Section 2 of the scoring model in Appendix A is designed specifically for this purpose. It allows executives and governance committees to assess whether implementation practices and leadership culture are functioning in practice rather than existing only as policy statements. The governance matrix in Appendix A helps identify whether the organization's combined governance and leadership profile is structurally sound, culturally sustained, or at risk of erosion under delivery pressure.

In mature organizations, these assessments become part of routine governance review cycles and executive reporting rather than one-time project exercises.

Why Leadership Determines Ethical Stability

The Five Pillars create structure.

The roadmap creates a process.

Leadership and ethical culture determine whether both endure.

Ethical stability is not sustained by documentation alone.

It is sustained by leadership discipline.

When leadership reinforces governance expectations, responsible AI becomes institutional practice.

When leadership signals that speed outweighs safeguards, governance erodes.

Responsible AI is ultimately a leadership commitment.

Leadership Self-Assessment Checklist

Ethical Culture and Tone

- ☐ Would we deploy this system if its limitations were made public?

- ☐ Do we reward teams for raising risks, or only for meeting delivery targets?

- ☐ Would we pause deployment if fairness results were uncertain?

- ☐ Do we treat responsible practice as part of project success, not as an obstacle to it?

Accountability and Oversight

- ☐ Is accountability clearly assigned at the executive level for each AI system?

- ☐ Do we monitor societal impacts or only financial outcomes?

- ☐ Do board-level reports cover risk classification, bias metrics, incidents, and regulatory developments?

Governance Maturity

- ☐ Has Section 2 of the AI Governance Readiness Scoring Model in Appendix A been completed at the leadership level?

- ☐ Has the governance matrix been used to assess whether leadership culture is sustaining or undermining governance structures?

- ☐ Are readiness assessments conducted as part of routine governance cycles, not only at project initiation?

Part V

Closing and References

Building Systems That Deserve Trust

From Capability to Responsibility

AI systems are powerful.

They shape decisions. They influence opportunities. They affect rights, markets, and social systems.

But capability alone does not define progress.

Power without accountability creates risk. Efficiency without governance creates instability. Innovation without oversight creates unintended harm.

The central argument of this book is simple:

AI project success must be redefined.

Redefining Success

Traditional project success measures focus on:

- Budgets

- Schedules

- Technical performance

- Business value

These remain important. But they are incomplete.

AI project success must also include:

- Stakeholder protection

- Clear accountability

- Transparency

- Continuous oversight

If a system performs well but harms vulnerable groups, it is not successful.

If it delivers financial return but violates regulatory obligations, it is not successful.

If it cannot be explained, monitored, or governed, it is not successful.

Success must include legitimacy.

The Five Pillars as Governance Infrastructure

The Five Pillars provide the structural foundation for moral AI projects:

- Governance anchors authority and accountability.

- Stakeholder inclusion ensures representation and impact awareness.

- Data responsibility safeguards legality, fairness, and quality.

- Transparency makes systems understandable and defensible.

- Long-term oversight sustains responsibility beyond deployment.

These pillars are not optional enhancements.

They are governance infrastructure.

Together, they transform ethics from aspiration into an operational discipline.

Regulation as Reinforcement, Not Replacement

Regulatory frameworks such as the EU AI Act and GDPR reinforce these expectations.

They require:

- Risk assessment

- Documentation

- Human oversight

- Transparency

- Post-market monitoring

But regulation alone cannot create an ethical culture.

Compliance avoids penalties. Governance builds trust.

Responsible AI requires both.

Leadership as the Deciding Factor

Structure matters. Processes matter. Documentation matters.

But leadership determines whether they endure.

Ethical AI is not achieved through checklists alone.

It is sustained when leaders:

- Reward responsible behavior

- Encourage risk escalation

- Accept transparency

- Balance innovation with protection

- Prioritize long-term legitimacy over short-term speed

Without leadership commitment, governance erodes under pressure.

With leadership discipline, governance becomes institutional.

Stewardship, Not Just Delivery

Autonomous systems do not automatically generate stronger accountability. Accountability must be intentionally built in proportion to system capability, context, and potential harm.

AI projects should not only deliver functional systems.

They must deliver systems that deserve trust.

This requires moving from a delivery mindset to a stewardship mindset.

Delivery asks:

- Does it work?

- Is it on time?

- Is it profitable?

Stewardship asks:

- Is it fair?

- Is it lawful?

- Is it explainable?

- Is it monitored?

- Can it be defended publicly?

Stewardship extends responsibility beyond system launch.

It treats AI systems as ongoing commitments requiring continuous oversight and accountability.

Ethical Stability as a Strategic Asset

Organizations that embed the Five Pillars create more than compliance.

They create:

- Durable trust

- Regulatory resilience

- Stronger stakeholder relationships

- Reduced reputational risk

- Sustainable innovation

Ethical stability becomes a competitive advantage.

In an environment of increasing scrutiny, responsible governance differentiates mature organizations from reactive ones.

The Leadership Decision

Responsible AI is ultimately a leadership decision.

It is a decision to:

- Define accountability clearly

- Invest in data discipline

- Include those affected

- Communicate transparently

- Monitor continuously

Technology will continue to evolve.

Regulation will continue to expand.

Public expectations will continue to rise.

The organizations that thrive will not be those that innovate fastest.

They will be those who innovate responsibly.

A Final Principle

Projects should not only deliver systems that work.

They must deliver systems that deserve trust.

Trust is not declared.

It is earned through governance, leadership, and sustained accountability.

Moral AI projects are not an aspiration.

They are a discipline.

The Five Pillars provide that discipline.

Appendix A: AI Governance Readiness Scoring Model

Purpose

This scoring model provides a structured maturity assessment aligned with the Five Pillars of Moral AI Projects and the implementation and leadership framework described in Chapters 16 and 17. It is designed for use during self-assessment, governance reviews, pre-deployment checkpoints, and executive oversight discussions.

The model is divided into two sections. Section 1 covers the Five Pillars. Section 2 covers implementation and leadership. Each section is scored independently so that strengths in one area do not mask weaknesses in another.

Each row is rated from 1 (Absent) to 5 (Institutionalized). Scoring should be based on documented evidence, not perception.

Scoring Scale

1: Absent	No formal structure; accountability undefined; controls not implemented.
2: Ad hoc	Informal or inconsistent practices; roles partially assigned; documentation incomplete.
3: Defined	Formal policies exist; responsibilities assigned; controls applied inconsistently.
4: Operational	Controls enforced in practice; documentation maintained; monitoring active.
5: Institutionalized	Governance embedded across lifecycle; executive oversight active; audit-ready and continuously improved.

Section 1: Five Pillars Assessment (Maximum 25)

Score	Interpretation
5–10	High Ethical Risk: Governance structures largely absent. Deployment of high-risk systems should pause.
11–18	Moderate Risk: Controls defined but inconsistently applied. Operational strengthening required.
19–22	Strong Governance: Operational maturity established; monitoring and documentation active.
23–25	Institutional Ethical Maturity: Governance embedded into organizational culture; audit-ready and strategically resilient.

Critical Rule: Five Pillars

If any single pillar scores 1, the overall system should be treated as high risk regardless of the total score. Ethical maturity requires balance across all five pillars.

Table A.1: Five Pillars Scoring Rubric aligned with the Five Pillars

1: Absent	2: Ad hoc	3: Defined	4: Operational	5: Institutional
Pillar: Governance				
No named executive accountability; no formal approval gates.	Roles partially assigned; ethical review inconsistent; escalation unclear.	Executive sponsor assigned; governance checkpoints defined but unevenly applied; decision rights and accountability mapping documented.	Formal review gates enforced; escalation routes active; documentation maintained; post-deployment ownership formally assigned.	Governance embedded across lifecycle; board visibility established; audit-ready oversight.
Pillar: Stakeholder Inclusion				
No structured stakeholder analysis; vulnerable groups not identified.	Stakeholders identified informally; no intersectional consideration; passive stakeholders not explicitly identified.	Stakeholder mapping completed; limited fairness testing across groups; stakeholder register maintained; representation mechanisms defined for low-voice groups.	Intersectional testing conducted; engagement budget allocated; monitoring includes subgroup impact; decision subjects explicitly identified and monitored.	Inclusion integrated into governance lifecycle; continuous stakeholder impact review.

Continued on next page

Table A.1 – continued from previous page

1: Absent	2: Ad hoc	3: Defined	4: Operational	5: Institutional
Pillar: Data Responsibility				
Data provenance undocumented; legal basis unclear; bias testing absent.	Basic compliance considered; inconsistent documentation; limited IP review.	Lawful basis documented; bias testing conducted but not systematically monitored; model card initiated with data characteristics and known limitations.	Data governance controls enforced; IP/licensing verified; DPIA conducted where required; annotation and labeling governance documented; quality controls in place.	Full traceability of data supply chain; continuous bias monitoring; independent audit capability; model card audit-ready and updated on retraining; personal agency considerations documented for all data collection contexts.
Pillar: Transparency & Explainability				
System logic undocumented; no user-level explanation provided.	Internal documentation exists; user transparency minimal.	Technical documentation maintained; basic explanation mechanisms available; model card completed and accessible to non-technical reviewers.	Audience-specific transparency packs implemented; limitations clearly communicated; decision challenge mechanisms available to affected individuals; GDPR right to explanation obligations met.	Transparency embedded into design standards; regulatory-ready documentation; periodic review; synthetic content disclosure obligations satisfied; model card reviewed and updated on material changes.

Continued on next page

Table A.1 – continued from previous page

1: Absent	2: Ad hoc	3: Defined	4: Operational	5: Institutional
Pillar: Long-Term Oversight				
No monitoring after deployment; no retraining governance.	Performance monitored informally; no structured incident management.	Monitoring plan documented; bias tracked periodically; retraining partially governed; monitoring cadence defined and documented.	Continuous monitoring implemented; incident reporting active; retraining governed formally; purpose creep controls in place; model card updated on retraining.	Post-market monitoring integrated into enterprise risk systems; executive reporting; defined shutdown triggers enforced.

Five Pillars Assessment: Pharmacy Facial Recognition Case

The following scores apply the Five Pillars Scoring Rubric to the pharmacy facial recognition case at the point of failure. They are theoretical assessments based on the documented failures described in the case and the FTC complaint, not an assessment of the organization's overall governance maturity. A well-governed version of this system could score significantly higher across all dimensions.

Table A.2: Five Pillars Assessment — Pharmacy Facial Recognition Case

Pillar	Score (1–5)	Key failure
Governance	1	No executive accountability; no approval gates; vendor claims unverified
Stakeholder Inclusion	1	No stakeholder analysis; customers unaware; no bias assessment across affected communities
Data Responsibility	1	Low-quality images; no consent controls; biometric data ungoverned; no bias testing
Transparency & Explainability	1	Customers not informed; employees not trained on system limits; no challenge mechanism
Long-Term Oversight	1	No post-deployment monitoring; false positive tracking absent or unenforced
Total	5 / 25	**High Ethical Risk**

Case Interpretation

The system scored at the lowest maturity level across all five pillars. Governance structures were absent, stakeholder groups were unidentified, data quality and consent controls were inadequate, transparency was withheld from both customers and employees, and post-deployment monitoring was either absent or unenforced. The total score of 5 out of 25 places the system firmly in the High Ethical Risk band. Under the critical rule above, a score of 1 on any single pillar is sufficient to classify the system as high risk regardless of the total score. In this case, every pillar scored 1.

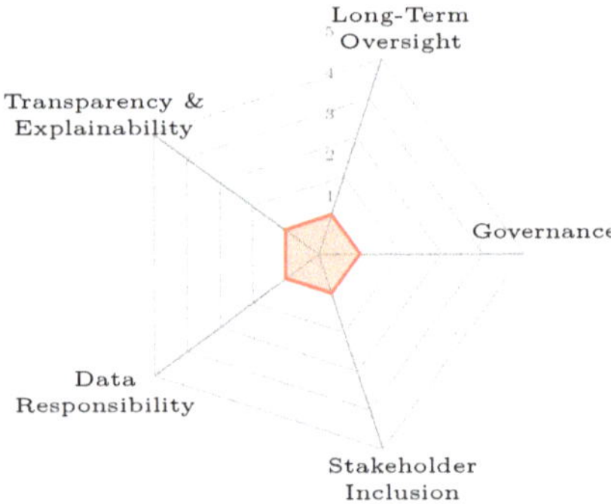

Figure A.1: Five Pillars Radar Diagram — Pharmacy Facial Recognition Case. All pillars scored 1 (Absent) at the point of failure. The shaded area represents the assessed governance profile.

Five Pillars Assessment: Four Case Studies

The following radar diagrams apply the Five Pillars Scoring Rubric to the four remaining case studies, scored at the point of failure as theoretical assessments based on documented governance failures.

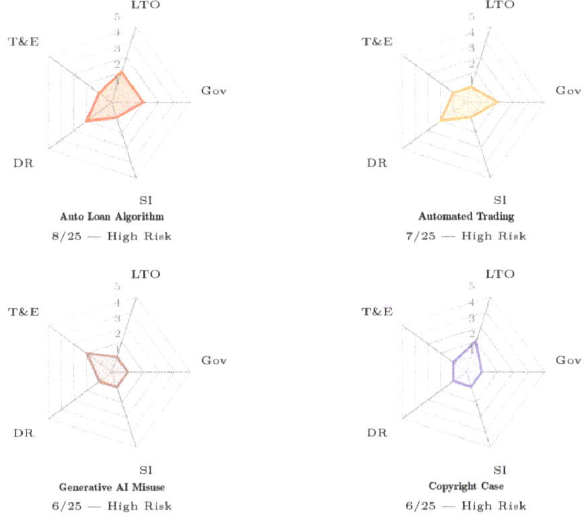

Gov = Governance   SI = Stakeholder Inclusion   DR = Data Responsibility
T&E = Transparency & Explainability   LTO = Long-Term Oversight

Figure A.2: Five Pillars radar diagrams for four case studies at the point of failure. All cases scored in the High Ethical Risk band (5–10). Scores are theoretical assessments based on documented governance failures and are not assessments of the organizations involved.

Section 2: Implementation and Leadership Assessment (Maximum 35)

Section 2 assesses the maturity of implementation practices and leadership culture that determine whether the governance structures evaluated in Section 1 are reliably sustained in practice. A strong Five Pillars score alongside a weak leadership score indicates that governance structures exist but may not endure under delivery pressure or organizational change.

Score Interpretation

7–14	High Risk: Implementation and leadership structures largely absent. Governance is unlikely to be sustained in practice.
15–24	Moderate Maturity: Structures partially defined. Leadership engagement inconsistent. Significant strengthening required.
25–30	Operational Maturity: Implementation embedded in project lifecycle; leadership actively supports governance.
31–35	Institutional Maturity: Responsible AI embedded in organizational culture; governance sustained across leadership changes and delivery pressure.

Critical Rule: Implementation and Leadership

If the Tone, Incentives, and Ethical Culture row or the Accountability and Diffusion Prevention row scores 1, the overall leadership assessment should be treated as high risk regardless of the total score. Governance structures cannot be sustained without active leadership reinforcement and clear accountability.

Table A.3: Implementation and Leadership Scoring Rubric aligned with the Roadmap and Governance

1: Absent	2: Ad hoc	3: Defined	4: Operational	5: Institutional
Implementation: Risk Classification and Concept Approval				
No risk classification conducted; EU AI Act category not assessed; governance structure undefined at project outset.	Risk classification attempted informally; GDPR implications considered inconsistently; governance structure partially defined.	EU AI Act risk category assessed and documented; GDPR implications reviewed; governance structure defined before development begins.	Risk classification verified by compliance function; stakeholder inclusion plan drafted at concept stage; budget allocated for governance controls.	Risk classification embedded in project initiation standards; independent review of high-risk classifications; governance controls funded and assigned before approval to proceed.
Implementation: Design and Data Preparation				
Decision rights undefined; data sourcing uncontrolled; no transparency planning at design stage.	Decision rights partially assigned; data sourcing considered informally; documentation checkpoints inconsistent.	Decision rights and approval gates documented; data sourcing controls established; bias testing protocols planned; transparency mechanisms identified.	RACI completed; lawful basis and licensing verified; DPIA conducted where required; documentation checkpoints enforced through ISO-aligned quality processes.	Design governance fully integrated into quality management system; data preparation audit-ready before development begins; independent fairness review conducted.

Continued on next page

Table A.3 – continued from previous page

1: Absent	2: Ad hoc	3: Defined	4: Operational	5: Institutional
Implementation: Development, Validation, and Pre-Deployment Gate				
No bias or robustness testing; model limitations undocumented; deployment approved without formal governance review.	Some testing conducted; documentation incomplete; deployment approval informal or inconsistent.	Bias and robustness testing conducted; model limitations documented; pre-deployment governance gate defined with sign-off authority identified.	Intersectional validation completed; technical documentation satisfies EU AI Act requirements; formal sponsor sign-off obtained before deployment; residual risks documented and accepted.	Pre-deployment gate embedded in project lifecycle standards; independent ethics review conducted for high-risk systems; conformity assessment completed where required; audit-ready documentation produced as standard.
Implementation: Deployment and Post-Market Monitoring				
No monitoring activated at deployment; no incident reporting channel; no usage controls defined.	Monitoring activated informally; incident reporting ad hoc; usage controls partially defined.	Monitoring plan activated at deployment; incident reporting channels established; usage controls and override procedures documented.	Monitoring cadence enforced; EU AI Act post-market obligations met; model card updated on retraining; serious incidents reported within required timeframes.	Post-market monitoring integrated into enterprise risk systems; executive reporting on performance, bias, and incidents established as routine; shutdown criteria enforced through formal governance process.

Continued on next page

Table A.3 – continued from previous page

1: Absent	2: Ad hoc	3: Defined	4: Operational	5: Institutional
Leadership: Tone, Incentives, and Ethical Culture				
Leadership does not engage with AI governance; delivery speed is the only recognized metric of success; ethical concerns are not raised or are ignored when raised.	Leadership acknowledges governance requirements but does not actively reinforce them; incentives favor delivery over responsible practice; ethical concerns raised informally but not consistently acted on.	Leadership visibly supports governance expectations; responsible behavior recognized alongside delivery performance; escalation of ethical concerns treated as acceptable practice.	Leadership regularly asks governance questions in project reviews; incentive structures explicitly recognize responsible practice; psychological safety for escalation is actively maintained; ethical drift identified and addressed when it occurs.	Ethical leadership embedded in organizational culture; governance performance included in executive accountability frameworks; responsible AI treated as a strategic commitment rather than a compliance obligation.

Leadership: Accountability, Diffusion Prevention, and Oversight

Continued on next page

Table A.3 – continued from previous page

1: Absent	2: Ad hoc	3: Defined	4: Operational	5: Institutional
Accountability for AI outcomes is unclear or assumed to belong to someone else; no named owner for critical decisions; board has no visibility of AI risk.	Accountability partially assigned; critical decisions made informally; board awareness of AI risk limited or occasional.	Accountability for critical decisions documented; named owners assigned for data governance, model validation, and deployment approval; board receives periodic AI risk reporting.	RACI maintained and reviewed at each project phase; diffusion of accountability actively managed; board receives regular reporting on risk classification, bias metrics, incidents, and regulatory developments.	Executive accountability for AI outcomes embedded in governance frameworks; board-level AI risk oversight established as standard practice; accountability assignments reviewed and updated as systems evolve.

Continued on next page

Table A.3 – continued from previous page

1: Absent	2: Ad hoc	3: Defined	4: Operational	5: Institutional
Leadership: Organizational Maturity and Continuous Improvement				
No governance review cycles; AI ethics treated as a one-time project activity; no lessons learned process.	Governance reviews occur reactively; lessons learned captured informally; ethical readiness tools not used consistently.	Governance review cycles defined; ethical readiness scoring conducted at key project gates; lessons learned documented after deployment.	Readiness scoring embedded in project lifecycle; continuous improvement cycle established; governance maturity assessed against defined indicators; cross-functional collaboration on AI ethics active.	AI governance treated as institutional infrastructure; readiness assessments feed into organizational improvement plans; independent oversight engaged for high-risk systems; ethical stability sustained across leadership changes and delivery pressure.

Implementation and Leadership Assessment: Pharmacy Facial Recognition Case

The implementation and leadership assessment for the pharmacy facial recognition case reflects the same pattern as the Five Pillars Assessment. Every dimension scored at the lowest level. Risk classification was not conducted, the system was deployed without validation or governance review, monitoring was absent or unenforced, and leadership culture neither required nor supported ethical governance practices. The FTC complaint documents that employees were actively discouraged from informing customers about the system, which is a direct indicator of a leadership culture that suppressed rather than supported transparency and accountability. The total score of 7 out of 35 places the system in the High Risk band, the lowest maturity classification in the implementation and leadership assessment.

Case Interpretation

Under the critical rule above, a score of 1 on either the Tone, Incentives, and Ethical Culture row or the Accountability and Diffusion Prevention row is sufficient to classify the leadership assessment as high risk regardless of the total score. In this case, both rows scored 1, and every other dimension scored 1 as well.

Table A.4: Implementation and Leadership Assessment — Pharmacy Facial Recognition Case

Dimension	Score (1–5)	Key failure
Risk Classification & Concept Approval	1	No risk classification; civil rights implications not assessed
Design & Data Preparation	1	Decision rights undefined; data sourcing uncontrolled; no transparency planning
Development, Validation, & Pre-Deployment Gate	1	No testing; vendor claims unverified; deployment without governance review
Deployment & Post-Market Monitoring	1	No monitoring; no incident reporting; usage controls absent or unenforced
Tone, Incentives, & Ethical Culture	1	Employees discouraged from transparency; ethical concerns not raised or acted on
Accountability, Diffusion Prevention, & Oversight	1	Accountability unclear; no named decision owners; no board visibility
Organizational Maturity & Continuous Improvement	1	No governance review cycles; no lessons learned process
Total	**7 / 35**	**High Risk**

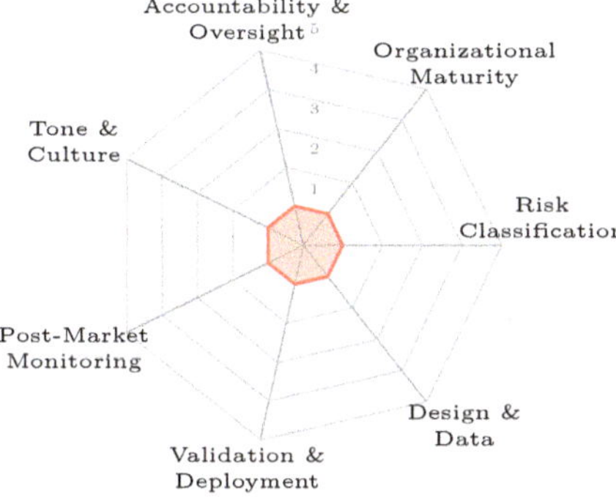

Figure A.3: Implementation and Leadership Radar — Pharmacy Facial Recognition Case. All seven dimensions scored 1 (Absent) at the point of failure.

Implementation and Leadership Assessment: Four Case Studies

The following radar diagrams apply the Implementation and Leadership Scoring Rubric to the four remaining case studies, scored at the point of failure as theoretical assessments based on documented governance failures.

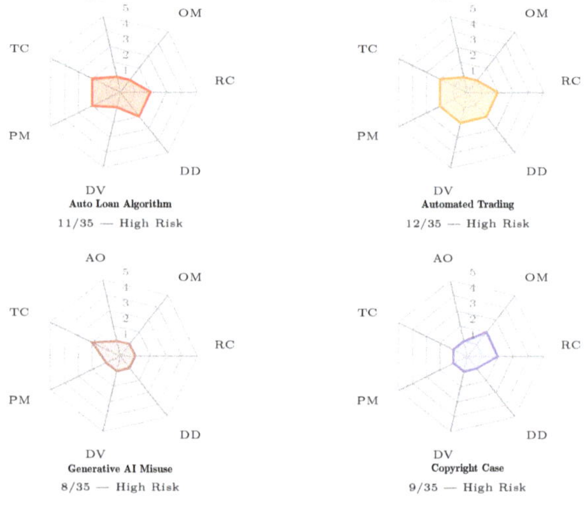

Figure A.4: Implementation and Leadership radar diagrams for four case studies at the point of failure. All cases scored in the High Risk band (7–14). Scores are theoretical assessments based on documented governance failures and are not assessments of the organizations involved.

Interpreting Combined Scores

The matrix below plots the Five Pillars score against the Implementation and Leadership score. Each quadrant describes a distinct governance profile. The case studies from this book are placed as theoretical examples of where organizations operating those systems might have scored at the point of failure.

Using Both Sections Together

A high Five Pillars score with a low leadership score suggests that governance structures are in place but may erode under pressure. The priority in this case is leadership development and cultural reinforcement.

A high leadership score with a low Five Pillars score suggests that leadership intent is present but has not yet been translated into operational governance structures. The priority in this case is implementing the controls described in the pillar chapters.

Balanced high scores across both sections indicate institutional ethical maturity: governance that is both structurally sound and culturally sustained.

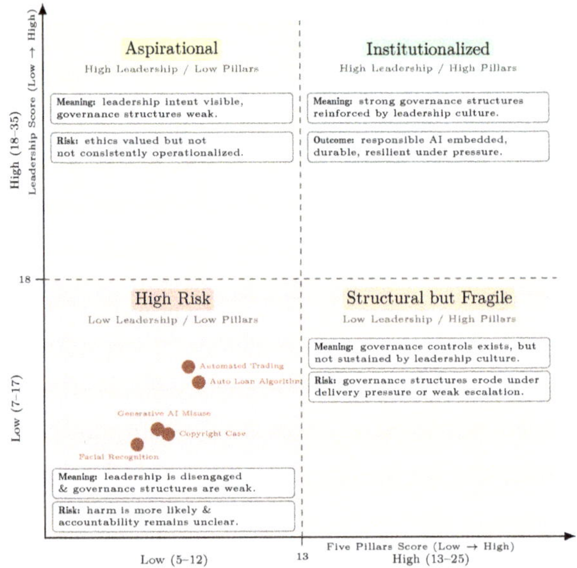

Note: case positions are theoretical illustrations based on the governance failures described in this book. They reflect the systems at the point of failure, not a full assessment of the organizations involved. A well-governed version of any of these systems could move into the Institutionalized quadrant.

Figure A.5: Leadership and Five Pillars Maturity Quadrant showing the relationship between leadership strength and operational governance maturity.

Appendix B: AI Ethical Readiness Scorecard

Purpose

This scorecard provides a structured self-assessment tool aligned with the Five Pillars of Moral AI Projects.

It is intended for use by:

- Project sponsors

- AI governance committees

- Risk and compliance teams

- Internal auditors

The scorecard does not replace formal regulatory assessment. It provides a governance maturity indicator.

AI Ethical Readiness Scorecard

One-page assessment aligned to the Five Pillars of Moral AI Projects (EU context).

How to use: Rate each pillar from **1 (Absent)** to **5 (Institutionalized)** using the maturity anchors below. Circle one score per row. Sum the total (max 25).

Maturity anchors (use as guidance)

1 Absent   2 Ad hoc   3 Defined   4 Operational   5 Institutionalized

Pillar and evidence cues	Score 1	2	3	4	5
Governance — Executive accountability assigned; approval gates documented; escalation route active; pre-deployment risk sign-off recorded.	○	○	○	○	○
Stakeholder Inclusion — Vulnerable and intersectional groups identified; engagement budgeted; representation built into data/validation; disproportionate impacts monitored.	○	○	○	○	○
Data Responsibility — Provenance and lawful basis documented; purpose limitation/minimization enforced; IP/licensing verified; bias testing recorded; audit trail maintained.	○	○	○	○	○
Transparency & Explainability — Audit-ready documentation; audience-specific transparency pack; limitations/uncertainty communicated; UI signals AI use; challenge route available.	○	○	○	○	○
Long-Term Oversight — Post-market monitoring plan; drift/bias tracked; re-training under change control; incident reporting active; shutdown/decommission criteria defined.	○	○	○	○	○

Total Score (max 25): _______________ Date: _______________

Project Manager _______________ Assessor: _______________

5–10: High Ethical Risk   Governance largely absent. Pause high-risk deployment and implement core controls before release.

11–18: Moderate Risk   Controls defined but inconsistent. Strengthen enforcement, documentation, and monitoring; re-score after remediation.

19–22: Strong Governance   Operational maturity established. Maintain cadence, audit readiness, and continuous improvement.

23–25: Institutional Ethical Maturity   Governance embedded across lifecycle with executive oversight and audit-ready evidence.

Critical rule: If any single pillar scores 1, treat the system as high risk regardless of total score.

Figure B.1: **Printable worksheet.** Photocopy or print for use

Appendix C: Stakeholder Identification and Inclusion Tool

This appendix provides a structured tool to support stakeholder identification and inclusion in AI projects.

AI systems affect stakeholders across multiple stages of the lifecycle: those who design systems, those who operate them, and those who experience their consequences. Some stakeholders may have little influence over the project yet face significant potential harm from system outcomes.

This tool helps project teams:

- Identify stakeholders across the AI lifecycle

- Assess stakeholder influence and potential harm

- Define representation mechanisms for low-voice groups

- Integrate stakeholder inclusion into governance checkpoints

Minimum Governance Rules

Each project should apply the following governance rules:

- Every AI project must maintain a stakeholder register.

- At least one group with *high harm and low influence* must be explicitly identified.

- Passive stakeholders must have a defined representation mechanism.

- Inclusion activities must be budgeted, not assumed.

- Stakeholder mapping must be reviewed at each major governance gate.

Step 1: Identify Stakeholders Across the AI Lifecycle

Stakeholders should be identified across three groups corresponding to their stage of interaction with the system.

- **Development stakeholders**: those who design and build the system, including project sponsors, project managers, engineers, data scientists, and legal and compliance teams.

- **Operational stakeholders**: those who interact with or operate the system, including end users, system operators, and system administrators.

- **External stakeholders**: individuals or groups affected by system outcomes, including decision subjects, workers, communities, regulators, and the general public.

Table C.1 illustrates common stakeholder roles across the development, operational, and external lifecycle stages. Projects should adapt this register to their specific system context.

Table C.1: Stakeholder Register (Example Roles)

Stakeholder / Group	Stage	Role	How the System Affects Them
Project Sponsor / Executive	Dev	A	Approves funding, risk tolerance, and deployment decisions.
Project Manager / Program Lead	Dev	A	Responsible for delivery, governance checkpoints, and coordination of technical and compliance activities.
AI Engineers / Data Scientists	Dev	A	Design models, select training data, and implement algorithms that determine system performance.
Legal / Compliance Team	Dev	A	Interpret regulatory requirements and ensure system design meets legal and governance obligations.
System Operators / Analysts	Ops	O	Use system outputs in workflows and may approve, review, or override automated decisions.
Business Users / Customer Service Staff	Ops	O	Depend on system recommendations to support operational decisions and customer interactions.
System Administrators / IT Operations	Ops	O	Responsible for system reliability, updates, retraining processes, and monitoring system performance.
Decision Subjects (Individuals evaluated by the system)	Ext	P	Receive outcomes generated by the AI system, such as approvals, rankings, or eligibility decisions.

Continued on next page

Table C.1 – continued from previous page

Stakeholder / Group	Stage	Role	How the System Affects Them
Customers / Clients	Ext	P	Experience the quality, fairness, and reliability of system decisions or recommendations.
Regulators / Supervisory Authorities	Ext	A	Oversee compliance with legal obligations and may investigate incidents or require corrective actions.
Civil Society / Advocacy Groups	Ext	P	Represent the interests of vulnerable populations or communities affected by system outcomes.
Affected Communities / Public	Ext	P	May experience indirect impacts such as fairness concerns, economic effects, or loss of trust.

Stage: Dev = Development; Ops = Operations; Ext = External

Role Type: A = Active; O = Operational; P = Passive

Step 2: Assess Stakeholder Attributes

Stakeholders should be evaluated using both traditional stakeholder attributes and AI-specific risk considerations.

Score each dimension from 1 to 5.

- **Power**: the ability to influence funding, approval, or continuation.

- **Legitimacy**: the strength of the stakeholder's claim to consideration.

- **Urgency**: how quickly concerns require attention.

- **Potential Harm**: the degree of potential negative impact if the system performs poorly.

- **Influence**: the ability to shape project decisions.

Stakeholders with *high potential harm and low influence* should receive particular attention in inclusion planning.

Step 3: Classify Stakeholder Roles

Stakeholders should be classified according to how they interact with the project.

- **Active stakeholders (A)** shape project decisions.

- **Operational stakeholders (O)** use or manage the system.

- **Passive stakeholders (P)** are affected by outcomes but have limited project power.

Passive stakeholders may require representation through regulators, community representatives, or advocacy organizations.

Step 4: Define Representation Mechanisms

For each stakeholder group, determine how representation will occur.

Table C.2: Stakeholder Representation Plan

Stakeholder	Engagement Type	Project Phase	Representative	Evidence
	Direct / Proxy	Concept / Design / Deployment		Meeting records, consultation notes, review memos

Step 5: Plan Stakeholder Inclusion

For each stakeholder group, define how inclusion will occur and estimate the resources required.

Table C.3: Stakeholder Inclusion Plan

Stake-holder	Inclusion Method	Repre-sentative / Proxy	Lifecycle Stage	Evidence	Estimated Inclusion Cost
	Workshop, consulta-tion, audit, survey				

Lifecycle Integration

Stakeholder inclusion should occur at key governance checkpoints.

Minimum Governance Expectations

Responsible AI projects should ensure that:

- A stakeholder register is maintained.

- High-impact stakeholders are identified early.

- Passive stakeholders receive representation when direct participation is not possible.

- Inclusion activities are budgeted and assigned to accountable owners.

- Stakeholder mapping is reviewed at major governance checkpoints.

Table C.4: Lifecycle Inclusion Map

Project Stage	Stakeholders Involved	Purpose
Concept and Scope	Sponsors, project team, affected stakeholders	Identify potential impacts and representation gaps
Data Preparation	Data team, domain experts, vulnerable populations	Assess representation and bias risks
Validation	Engineers, users, regulators, specialized groups	Evaluate fairness, usability, and safety
Pre-Deployment Governance Gate	Executives, compliance, representatives	Confirm readiness and unresolved risks
Post-Deployment Monitoring	Operators, oversight bodies, affected stakeholders	Detect disproportionate impacts and unintended consequences

Appendix D: Dataset Governance Assessment

Purpose

The Dataset Governance Assessment is a structured checklist for evaluating whether a dataset is appropriate, responsibly collected, sufficiently documented, and fit for purpose before it is used in an AI system.

It is designed to be used alongside the Dataset Governance worksheet in Appendix E. The worksheet provides a one-page structured template for recording decisions and evidence. This checklist provides the questions to ask and answer when working through each section of the template. The two documents share the same numbered structure so that checklist items map directly to worksheet sections.

Together, they cover dataset details, intended purpose, out-of-scope uses, ethical trade-offs, composition and representativeness, collection and legal basis, processing and labeling, personal agency and data subject rights, lifecycle maintenance, and governance sign-off.

Completing both documents creates a traceable, audit-ready record of the governance decisions made about a dataset before model training begins. This record supports regulatory review under the EU AI Act and GDPR, provides evidence for the readiness scoring process in Appendix A, and connects directly to the model card in Appendix E, which documents how the system behaves when trained on that data.

Evaluation should be based on documented evidence, not perception. If a question cannot be answered with reference to a document, record, or named decision-maker, the governance gap it reveals should be resolved before the dataset is approved for use.

Dataset Governance Assessment

1) Dataset Details

☐ Who created the dataset and on whose behalf?

☐ What version is it?

☐ What are the owner, date, source, and contact?

☐ What licenses apply?

☐ Where is the related documentation located?

2) Purpose and Intended Use

☐ What decision or system does this dataset support?

☐ What problem or gap does it address?

☐ What are the intended and permitted use cases?

3) Out-of-Scope Uses

☐ What uses are not appropriate or carry elevated risk?

☐ What harms could arise from misuse or out-of-scope application?

☐ What mitigation measures are required for safe use?

Continued

Assessment Continued

4) Ethical Trade-Offs

☐ Does improving representation require intrusive data collection or surveillance?

☐ Are alternative approaches available, such as synthetic data, proxies, or consultation?

☐ Do trade-offs consider impacts on data subject rights and human dignity?

5) Composition and Representativeness

☐ What populations or groups are included?

☐ Which groups are underrepresented or missing, and why?

☐ Have intersectional groups been considered and tested for bias?

☐ Are there known errors, gaps, or sources of noise?

Continued

Assessment Continued

6) Collection, Provenance, and Legal Basis

☐ How was the data collected, including source, method, and timeframe?

☐ Is the legal basis clearly defined, and were individuals informed where required?

☐ Does the dataset include copyrighted works, and do licenses explicitly permit the intended use?

☐ Are regulatory constraints, cross-border transfer requirements, and DPIA obligations identified and addressed?

7) Processing, Labeling, and Scale

☐ What preprocessing, cleaning, or transformation was performed, and are assumptions documented?

☐ Who performed labeling or annotation, and what instructions guided them?

☐ Are quality controls in place for labeling consistency, accuracy, and sensitive category handling?

☐ Is the dataset size justified relative to measurable improvements in fairness, accuracy, or safety, and are environmental costs considered?

Continued

Assessment Continued

8) Personal Agency and Data Subject Rights

☐ Can individuals realistically refuse data collection, and are opt-out mechanisms accessible?

☐ Can individuals access, correct, or delete their data?

☐ Can individuals challenge outcomes or request human review?

☐ Are vulnerable groups disproportionately exposed to collection or harm?

9) Maintenance and Lifecycle

☐ Who is responsible for maintaining the dataset, and how are updates and corrections managed?

☐ Are retention and deletion policies defined and enforced?

☐ How are users or downstream teams informed of changes or issues?

☐ Is the model card updated when the dataset changes?

10) Governance Decision and Sign-Off

☐ Is the dataset fit for its stated purpose, and is additional data required or should collection be limited?

☐ What risks require mitigation before use, and what controls or restrictions must be applied?

☐ Who reviewed this assessment?

☐ Who is accountable for approval and sign-off?

Appendix E: AI System Documentation Worksheets

Purpose

Responsible AI governance requires more than good intentions. It requires documentation that is structured, consistent, and audit-ready across the full system lifecycle.

This appendix provides four one-page worksheets that together create a record of how an AI system is designed, built, deployed, and monitored. Each worksheet can be used independently, but they are most effective when used together. Completed as a set, they provide the kind of traceable, cross-referenced documentation that governance reviews, pre-deployment gates, and regulatory inspections require.

The four worksheets are:

- **Dataset Governance** — documents the origin, composition, legal basis, and governance controls for datasets used to train or operate the system

- **Model Card** — documents model purpose, performance, limitations, bias testing results, and validated use cases

- **User Interface Synopsis** — documents how the system is presented to users, what they are expected to understand, and where misunderstanding or misuse could occur

- **Oversight** — documents how the system will be monitored, governed, and, if necessary, decommissioned after deployment

Together with Appendix C, which provides the Stakeholder Identification and Inclusion Tool, these worksheets support all five pillars: governance, stakeholder inclusion, data responsibility, transparency and explainability, and long-term oversight.

Scope and Limitations

These worksheets are designed for practical use in project workshops, governance reviews, and pre-deployment checkpoints. They provide concise, standardized summaries rather than a replacement for detailed technical documentation. Where fuller technical records are required — for example, to satisfy EU AI Act documentation obligations for high-risk systems — these worksheets should be accompanied by the complete technical documentation described in Chapters 5–9.

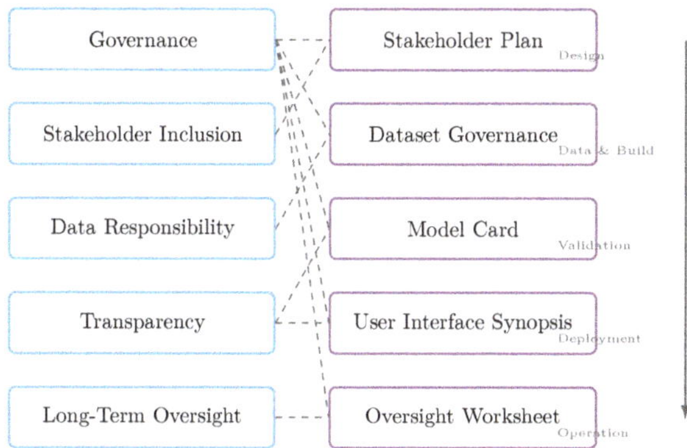

Figure E.1: Worksheet Ecosystem Across the Five Pillars shows the relationship between the five pillars and the practical worksheets used to apply them across the AI lifecycle.

When to Use Each Worksheet

- The **Dataset Governance** worksheet is used during data sourcing, preparation, and approval, before model training begins.

- The **Model Card** is completed before deployment and updated whenever the model is retrained or its performance materially changes.

- The **User Interface Synopsis** is used during interface design, testing, and pre-deployment review.

- The **Oversight** worksheet is completed before deployment and reviewed at each post-market monitoring checkpoint.

Each worksheet should have a named owner responsible for preparing it, a named reviewer, and a named approver. An undated or unsigned worksheet is incomplete as a governance document.

Dataset Governance

The Dataset Governance worksheet documents a dataset's origin, composition, intended use, and governance controls before it is used in an AI system. It helps teams assess whether data is appropriate, responsibly collected, sufficiently documented, and fit for purpose. It also addresses whether data collection respects personal agency, particularly in environments where legal protections are weak or inconsistently applied.

This worksheet combines the concept of datasheets for datasets (Gebru et al., 2018) with stakeholder and data governance considerations into a practical tool that supports transparency, accountability, and informed decision-making throughout the data lifecycle.

The Dataset Governance worksheet and the Model Card are complementary documents. The dataset worksheet explains what data is and where it comes from. The model card explains how the system behaves when trained on that data. Together they provide a traceable account of both the inputs and the outputs of the AI development process.

The corresponding Dataset Governance Assessment checklist in Appendix D guides the questions to consider when working through each section of this worksheet.

Model Card

The Model Card documents AI model behavior in a form that is visible, reviewable, and accountable across stakeholder groups. It is not a technical artifact intended only for engineering teams. It is a structured summary designed to support communication, decision-making, and accountability across the full AI lifecycle.

A well-prepared model card helps answer the questions that governance reviews, deployment gates, and regulatory inspections are most likely to ask:

- What is this model intended to do?

- What data was used to train and evaluate it?

- How does it perform across different conditions and groups?

- Where are its limitations and risks?

- What safeguards are required for responsible use?

A completed model card provides documented evidence relevant to the readiness scoring process in Appendix A, supports the stakeholder inclusion requirements described in Appendix C, and records the data governance decisions assessed in Appendix D and the dataset worksheet in this appendix.

One-Page Dataset Governance

Use this worksheet to document dataset purpose, composition, collection, governance, and lifecycle controls.
Source: adapted from Gebru et al. (2018)

1) Dataset details   Name   Version   Owner   Date   Source   Contact   License   Documentation location

2) Purpose and intended use
System supported
Problem addressed
Permitted use cases

3) Out-of-scope uses
Inappropriate uses
Misuse harms
Mitigation measures

4) Ethical trade-offs
Inclusion risks
Alternatives considered
Rights and dignity impacts

5) Composition and representativeness   Groups included, underrepresented populations, intersectional coverage, and known gaps

Groups included	Groups missing	Intersectional gaps	Errors / noise

6) Collection, provenance, and legal basis   How data was collected, legal basis, IP and copyright, cross-border transfers, & impact

Collection method	Legal basis / consent	IP / copyright	Constraints / DPIA

7) Processing, labeling, and scale   Preprocessing steps, labeling, quality controls, size justification, & environmental costs

Preprocessing	Labeling / annotation	Quality controls	Scale justification

8) Personal agency and data subject rights   Consent, opt-out, access / correction rights, challenge mechanisms, & vulnerable group exposure

Consent / opt-out	Access / correction	Challenge mechanisms	Vulnerable groups

9) Maintenance and lifecycle
Updates and corrections
Retention and deletion
Change notification
Model card update trigger

10) Governance decision and sign-off
Fit for purpose decision
Risks and controls
Reviewer
Accountable approver

Tip: Update this datasheet whenever the dataset, source, preprocessing steps, or governance constraints change.

Figure E.2: **Printable worksheet.** One-Page Dataset Governance.

The model card must be updated whenever the model is retrained, whenever material changes in performance are detected during post-deployment monitoring, or whenever the deployment context or intended use changes. An outdated model card is a governance gap.

User Interface Synopsis

The User Interface Synopsis documents how an AI system is presented to users, what they are expected to understand, and where misunderstanding or misuse could occur (Albrecht, 2013).

The interface is where governance becomes visible to the people the system affects. It is the point at which users interpret outputs, act on recommendations, and experience the system's limitations in practice. A system that is well governed internally but poorly communicated at the interface level has not achieved meaningful transparency.

This worksheet is used during interface design, testing, and pre-deployment review to ensure that the interface clearly communicates system purpose, limitations, and risks, and that appropriate safeguards, feedback mechanisms, and accountability structures are in place.

Key questions the synopsis should address include whether users are told that AI is involved, whether outputs are clearly distinguished as recommendations or binding decisions, whether confidence levels and uncertainty are communicated, and whether users have a clear route to question or challenge a decision.

One-Page Model Card

Use this worksheet to document model purpose, performance, limits, and governance-relevant cautions.
Source: adapted from Mitchell et al. (2019)

1) Model details

Name, version, owner, date, model type, contact, license, and related documentation

2) Intended use

Who should use it, for what decision, and in what setting.

3) Out-of-scope use

Where the model should not be used or trusted.

4) Factors, metrics, and data — Demographic or phenotypic groups, environmental conditions, technical attributes, etc.

Factors	Metrics	Training data	Evaluation data

5) Quantitative analyses — Summarize key results across relevant groups, contexts, or intersectional categories

Group / condition	Metric 1	Metric 2	Metric 3	Notes

6) Ethical considerations

Who may be harmed, fairness concerns, sensitive uses.

7) Caveats and recommendations

Known limitations, required safeguards, and follow-up actions.

Tip: Update this card when the model, data, thresholds, or deployment context changes.

Figure E.3: **Printable worksheet.** One-page model card template for documenting intended use, data, performance, ethical considerations, and deployment cautions.

One-Page User Interface Synopsis

Use this worksheet to document interface purpose, transparency, user understanding, and governance risks.
Source: adapted from Albrecht (2013)

1) System and interface identification

Name, version, provider, contact, deployment context, platform

2) Purpose and intended use

What the interface does, who uses it, and
what decisions it supports

3) User groups and context

User roles, skill level, environment, and constraints

4) Interface functionality and interaction

Inputs	Outputs	User actions	System behavior

5) Transparency, explanation, and limits   What users are told, what is hidden, and what may be misunderstood

What is explained	What is not explained	Limits and uncertainty	User risks

6) Data use and privacy

What data is collected, shown, stored, or shared

7) Governance, feedback, and escalation

Who is accountable, how issues are reported, and
how users challenge outcomes

Tip: Review this synopsis during design, testing, and before deployment to ensure users are not misled.

Figure E.4: **Printable worksheet.** One-page interface synopsis for documenting user-facing behavior, transparency, risks, and governance.

Oversight Worksheet

The Oversight Worksheet helps project teams define how an AI system will be monitored, governed, and if necessary decommissioned after deployment. It translates the long-term oversight requirements described in Chapter 9 into a structured, auditable record.

The worksheet covers four core areas:

- **Ongoing data protection**: ensuring that GDPR obligations, retention policies, and purpose limitations continue to be met after deployment

- **Benefits and protections in balance**: evaluating whether the system's operational benefits remain aligned with protections for the people it affects

- **Societal and environmental impacts**: reviewing broader consequences including labor displacement, energy consumption, and structural inequality

- **Shutdown and decommissioning criteria**: defining the conditions under which the system should be modified, suspended, or permanently decommissioned

This worksheet should be completed before deployment and reviewed at each post-market monitoring checkpoint. Completing it helps ensure that responsibility does not end at launch but continues throughout the system's operational lifecycle.

One-Page Oversight

Define monitoring, accountability, and escalation after deployment.

1) System and deployment context

2) Monitoring cadence

Frequency	What to monitor	Owner

3) Usage controls and human oversight

4) Retraining and change governance

5) Incident reporting and escalation

6) Shutdown and decommissioning

Tip: Oversight is continuous. Update this plan whenever the system, data, or use case changes.

Figure E.5: **Printable worksheet.** Use during deployment planning and governance reviews.

Bibliography

Albrecht, U.-V. (2013). Transparency of health-apps for trust and decision making. *J. Med. Internet Res.*, *15*(12), 1–5. https://doi.org/10.2196/jmir.2981

Bartz v. Anthropic PBC. (2025, July).

Batchelar v. Interactive Brokers, LLC. (2019).

Bender, E. M., Gebru, T., McMillan-Major, A., & Mitchell, M. (2021). On the dangers of stochastic parrots: Can language models be too big? *FAccT 2021: Proc. 2021 ACM Conf. Fairness Account. Transpar.*, 610–623. https : / / doi . org / 10 . 1145 / 3442188 . 3445922

Chasalow, K., & Levy, K. (2021). Representativeness in statistics, politics, and machine learning. *FAccT '21: Proceedings of the 2021 ACM Conference on Fairness, Accountability, and Transparency*, 77–89. https://doi.org/10.1145/3442188.3445872

European Commission. (2016). General data protection regulation.

European Union. (2024). Regulation (EU) 2024/1689 of the European Parliament and of the Council of 13 June 2024 laying down harmonised rules on artificial intelligence and amending Regulations

(EC) No 300/2008, (EU) No 167/2013, (EU) No 168/2013, (EU) 2018/858, (EU) 2018/1139 and (EU) 2019/2144 and Directives 2014/90/EU, (EU) 2016/797 and (EU) 2020/1828 (Artificial Intelligence Act). http://data.europa.eu/eli/reg/2024/1689/oj

FTC. (2023). Rite aid banned from using AI facial recognition after FTC says retailer deployed technology without reasonable safeguards. https://www.ftc.gov/

Gebru, T., Morgenstern, J., Vecchione, B., Vaughan, J. W., Wallach, H., Daumé III, H., & Crawford, K. (2018). Datasheets for datasets. *arXiv preprint*. https://arxiv.org/abs/1803.09010v7

International Standards Organization. (2023). ISO/IEC 42001: 2023-12 information technology – artificial intelligence – management system first edition.

Mata v. Avianca, Inc. (2023, June).

Miller, G. J. (2022a). Artificial intelligence project success factors-beyond the ethical principles. In E. Ziemba & W. Chmielarz (Eds.), *Information technology for management: Business and social issues. Fed-CSIS - AIST 2021/ISM 2021. lecture notes in business information processing* (pp. 65–96, Vol. 442). Springer.

Miller, G. J. (2022b). Stakeholder roles in artificial intelligence projects. *Proj. Leadersh. Soc., 3, Art. no. 100068*. https://doi.org/10.1016/j.plas.2022.100068

Miller, G. J. (2022c). Stakeholder-accountability model for artificial intelligence projects. *J. Econ. Manag.*, *44*(1), 446–494. https://doi.org/10.22367/jem.2022.44.18

Miller, G. J. (2025a). Framework for managing artificial intelligence (AI) projects: Avoiding harms, losses, and damages. In K. D. Strang & N. R. Vajjhala (Eds.), *International program and project management best practices in selected industries* (pp. 135–162). Springer Nature Switzerland. https://doi.org/10.1007/978-3-031-80275-1_7

Miller, G. J. (2025b). Level of automation and accountability in artificial intelligence (AI) projects: An empirical study. *2025 IEEE Technology and Engineering Management Society Conference - Global (TEMSCON Global)*, 1–6. https://doi.org/10.1109/TEMSCONGlobal64363.2025.11238326

Miller, G. J. (2025c). Simultaneous pursuit of accountability for regulatory compliance, financial benefits, and societal impacts in artificial intelligence (AI) projects. *2025 20th Conference on Computer Science and Intelligence Systems (FedCSIS)*, 207–217. https://doi.org/10.15439/2025F6392

Mitchell, M., Wu, S., Zaldivar, A., Barnes, P., Vasserman, L., Hutchinson, B., Spitzer, E., Raji, I. D., & Gebru, T. (2019). Model cards for model reporting. *FAT* 2019 - Proc. 2019 Conf. Fairness Account. Transpar.*, 220–229. https://doi.org/10.1145/3287560.3287596

Sheridan, T., & Verplank, W. (1978, March). *Human and computer control of undersea teleoperators* (Report). Massachusetts Institute of Technology. Cambridge, MA, USA.

Tabassi, E. (2023, January). Artificial intelligence risk management framework (AI RMF 1.0). https://doi.org/10.6028/NIST.AI.100-1

Walter Auto Loan Tr. v. Track Motors, LLC. (2023, August).

Glossary

Accountability The obligation of individuals or organizations to take responsibility for the outcomes of their decisions and actions, especially when harm occurs

Accountability Diffusion A situation where responsibility for decisions or outcomes becomes spread across many individuals or groups, making it unclear who is ultimately responsible

Algorithm A step-by-step set of instructions that a computer follows to process data and produce a result or decision

Artificial Intelligence (AI) Computer systems designed to perform tasks that normally require human intelligence, such as learning, reasoning, or decision-making

Autonomy (in AI) The ability of an AI system to operate or make decisions without direct human control

Bias (Data Bias) Systematic errors in data that cause an AI system to produce unfair or inaccurate results for certain groups

Data Governance The set of policies, roles, and processes that ensure data is accurate, secure, ethical, and properly managed

Data Subject A person whose data is collected, stored, or used to train or operate an AI system

Decision Subject A person directly affected by the output of an AI system, such as someone denied a loan or rejected for a job

Decision-Making System An AI system that influences or makes choices that affect individuals, organizations, or society

Ethical Drift The gradual weakening of ethical governance practices as small compromises accumulate and become accepted norms. Ethical drift typically begins when delivery timelines, cost pressures, or competing priorities lead to governance steps being deferred or skipped. Over time, those deferrals redefine what teams consider acceptable, eroding the governance discipline established at the outset of a project.

Ethical Intensity The degree to which a decision or action has the potential to cause significant moral consequences for individuals or society

Ethical Principles Guidelines such as fairness, transparency, and responsibility that help determine whether an AI system behaves in an acceptable way

European Union Artificial Intelligence Act (EU AI Act) A binding European Union regulation establishing a risk-based legal framework for Artificial Intelligence systems.

Explainability The ability to clearly describe how and why an AI system made a particular decision

GOVERN–MAP–MEASURE–MANAGE Core functional structure of the NIST AI Risk Management Framework

Governance The framework of rules, roles, and oversight structures that guide how an AI project is managed and controlled

Governance Checkpoint A formal review point in a project where risks, compliance requirements, and ethical considerations are evaluated before the project moves forward

Information Asymmetry A situation where one party in a project has more or better information than another, which can create risk or unfair advantage

Institutional Accountability Responsibility embedded within organizational rules, roles, and governance systems rather than relying solely on individual judgment

International Electrotechnical Commission An international standards organization that develops and publishes global standards for electrical, electronic, and related technologies. In the context of AI governance, IEC collaborates with ISO to develop joint standards such as ISO/IEC 42001 for Artificial Intelligence management systems.

Machine Learning A type of AI where systems learn patterns from data and improve their performance over time without being explicitly programmed for every task

Moral Disengagement A psychological process in which individuals distance themselves from the ethical consequences of their actions, often by viewing decisions as purely technical or procedural

Moral Hazard A risk that occurs when one party takes actions without bearing the full consequences of those actions

NIST AI Risk Management Framework (NIST AI RMF) A voluntary framework published by the U.S. National Institute of Standards and Technology (NIST) that provides structured guidance for identifying, assessing, managing, and governing risks associated with Artificial Intelligence systems.

Project Governance The system of leadership, oversight, and control that ensures a project meets its objectives responsibly

Project Sponsor The person or organization that provides funding and strategic direction for a project

Purpose Creep The gradual expansion of how a technology or dataset is used beyond its original purpose, often without sufficient review, consent, or governance

Responsibility Redirection The shifting of responsibility for outcomes to other individuals, teams, systems, or external actors rather than accepting direct accountability

Social Drift The gradual normalization of practices that initially appear questionable or risky, often occurring when teams repeatedly bypass safeguards to meet deadlines or performance targets

Stakeholder Any individual or group that is affected by, or can influence, an AI system or project

Stakeholder Theory A theory that argues organizations should consider the interests of all affected parties, not just shareholders or paying clients

Structural Accountability Accountability reinforced through formal governance mechanisms such as defined roles, review processes, approval authorities, and documented decision records

Structural Tension A situation where organizational goals, incentives, or processes create pressure that conflicts with ethical governance or responsible decision-making

Transparency The practice of openly sharing information about how an AI system works, including its limits and risks

Trust (in AI) Confidence that an AI system will operate reliably, fairly, and safely over time

Unintended Consequences Outcomes that were not planned or expected when an AI system was designed or deployed

Validation The process of testing an AI system to confirm that it performs accurately and as intended

Value Creation The measurable benefits an AI system provides, such as efficiency, cost savings, improved decision-making, or social good

Acronyms

AI Artificial Intelligence

APM Association for Project Management

EU European Union

IEC International Electrotechnical Commission

ISO International Organization for Standardization

NIST National Institute of Standards and Technology

RMF Risk Management Framework

Index

E

U

V

W